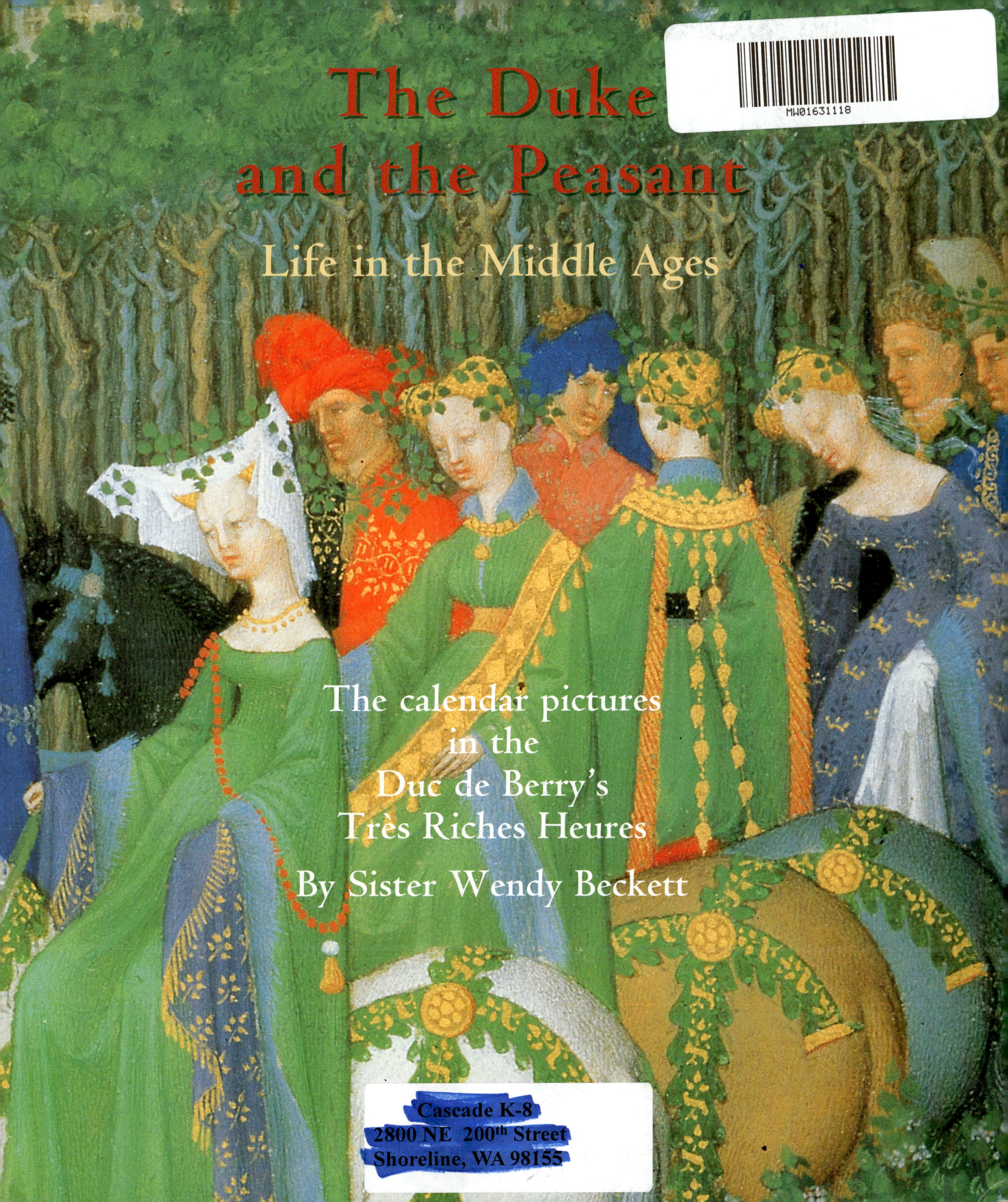

The Duke and the Peasant

Life in the Middle Ages

The calendar pictures in the Duc de Berry's Très Riches Heures

By Sister Wendy Beckett

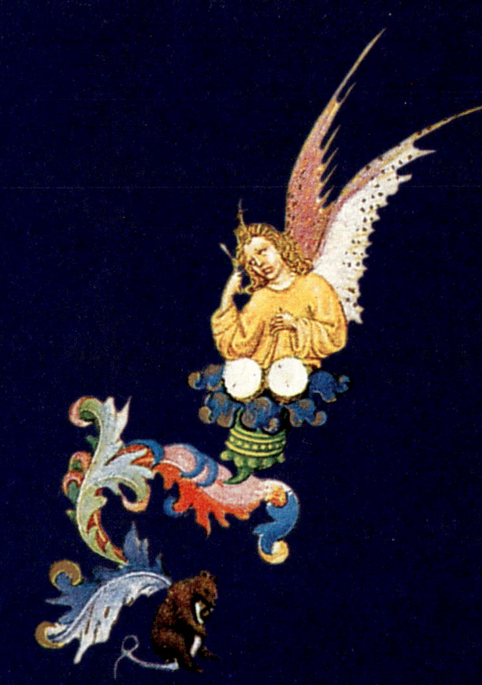

The Duc de Berry's Book of Hours

About 500 years ago, everybody went to church. If they were rich, they liked to have a special prayer book, called a Book of Hours, with prayers for every third hour of the day, when the monks and nuns went to pray. If they were very rich, this prayer book was splendidly illustrated — and one of the very richest of all was the Duc de Berry. He had fifteen Books of Hours, some, like the *Très Riches Heures*, too big actually to take to church, but very beautiful to look at. Whether he prayed from these books or just enjoyed the art, is his business, not ours. What is our own business is to enjoy the beautiful book he has left behind for us.

Books of Hours did not only have religious pictures, though, of course, they had those too. At the beginning, they actually had a Calendar, twelve paintings of the months of the year, when the artists could really show their appreciation of nature and the world around them. The calendar pictures in the *Très Riches Heures* depict the life of peasants and nobles in the Middle Ages.

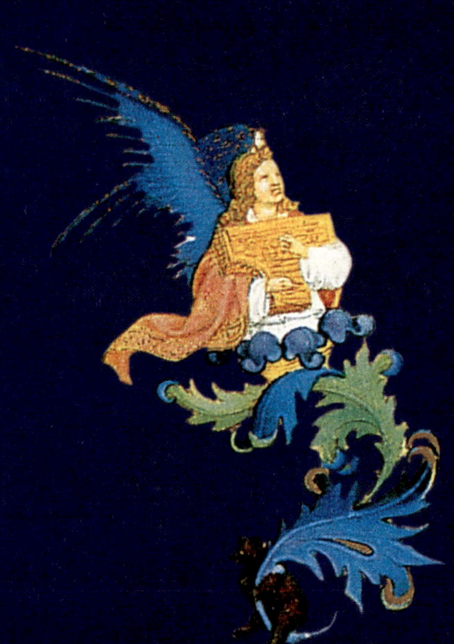

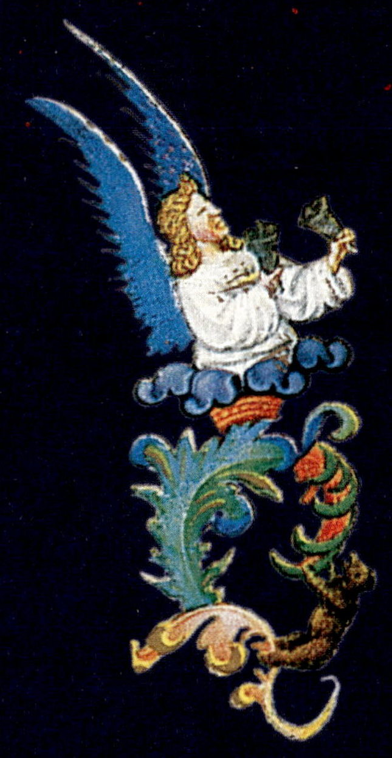

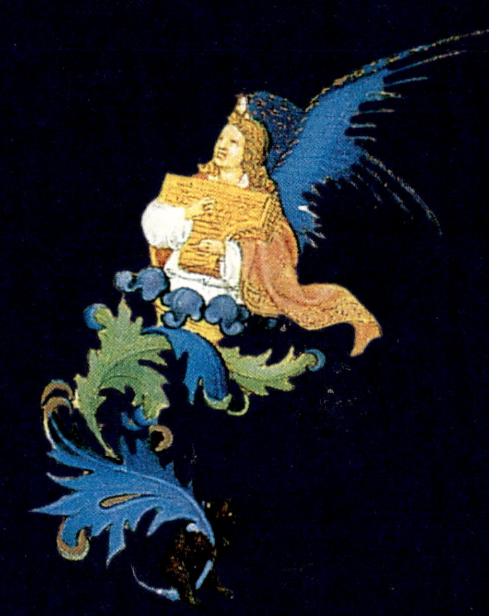

The Duc de Berry had three famous artists working for him — the Limbourg brothers. The oldest was probably Pol, whom we would call Paul, and then there was Jehanequin (Johnny), and Hermann. They were young men, and they all died suddenly around 1416, the same year as the duke's death, which makes us think they may all have caught the plague. When they died, the *Très Riches Heures* was not finished, and other artists had to complete it. If you look closely at these twelve months of the year, you will come to recognize which paintings are by the three Limbourgs and which are not. There is something extra, a magical touch about their work, although the other pictures are lovely, too.

Because the earth moves round the sun, each month has a different pattern of stars in the sky, the Zodiac as it is called. So above each picture the artists painted the right 'sign of the Zodiac'. February, for example, has the sign of the Watercarrier, Aquarius, giving way to the Fish, Pisces, with the Chariot of the Sun in the middle, while October passes from the Scales, Libra, to the Scorpion. But these are just added to the painting, it is the painting itself that matters.

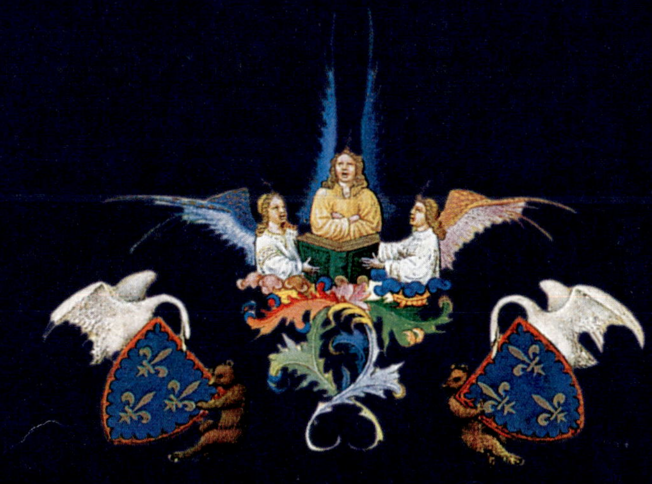

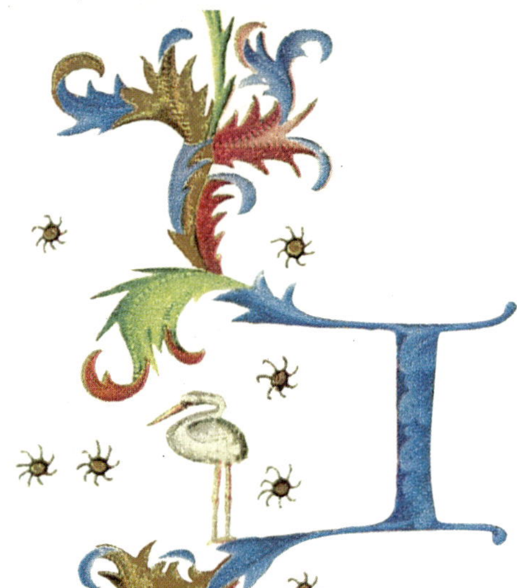

January

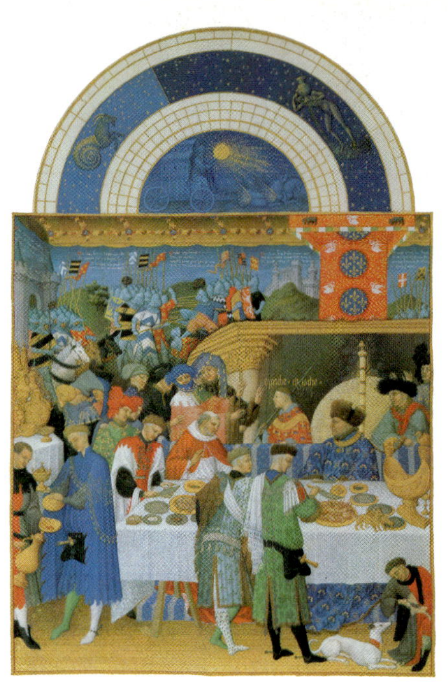

January shows the Duc de Berry having his New Year party. He is dressed in blue for the festivities and everything in the picture is meant to tell us how rich and important he is. But is it really a party, when only one other person is allowed to sit down? And even he, the bishop, has to sit right at the end of the bench, because the duke is far too important to have anybody near him. All the others here are friends and relatives or work for the duke as waiters, secretaries or soldiers. He has dressed them all in wonderful clothes, and he has had his table laid with solid gold dishes and jugs, including a golden ship for the salt. The walls are hung with a magnificent tapestry depicting knights in a battle. The duke is the CENTRE. But look at his face. He may be wearing a great diamond in his hat and a golden collar, but his mouth is turned down and he seems so glum. He has tiny dogs on his table, but he has no time to look at them, or at the wonderful hunting dog in the front. Here in his great hall he is not bothered by the soldiers fighting, but he has brought worries inside with him, inside his head. Perhaps the artists are asking: is it such fun, after all, to be very rich and the most important person?

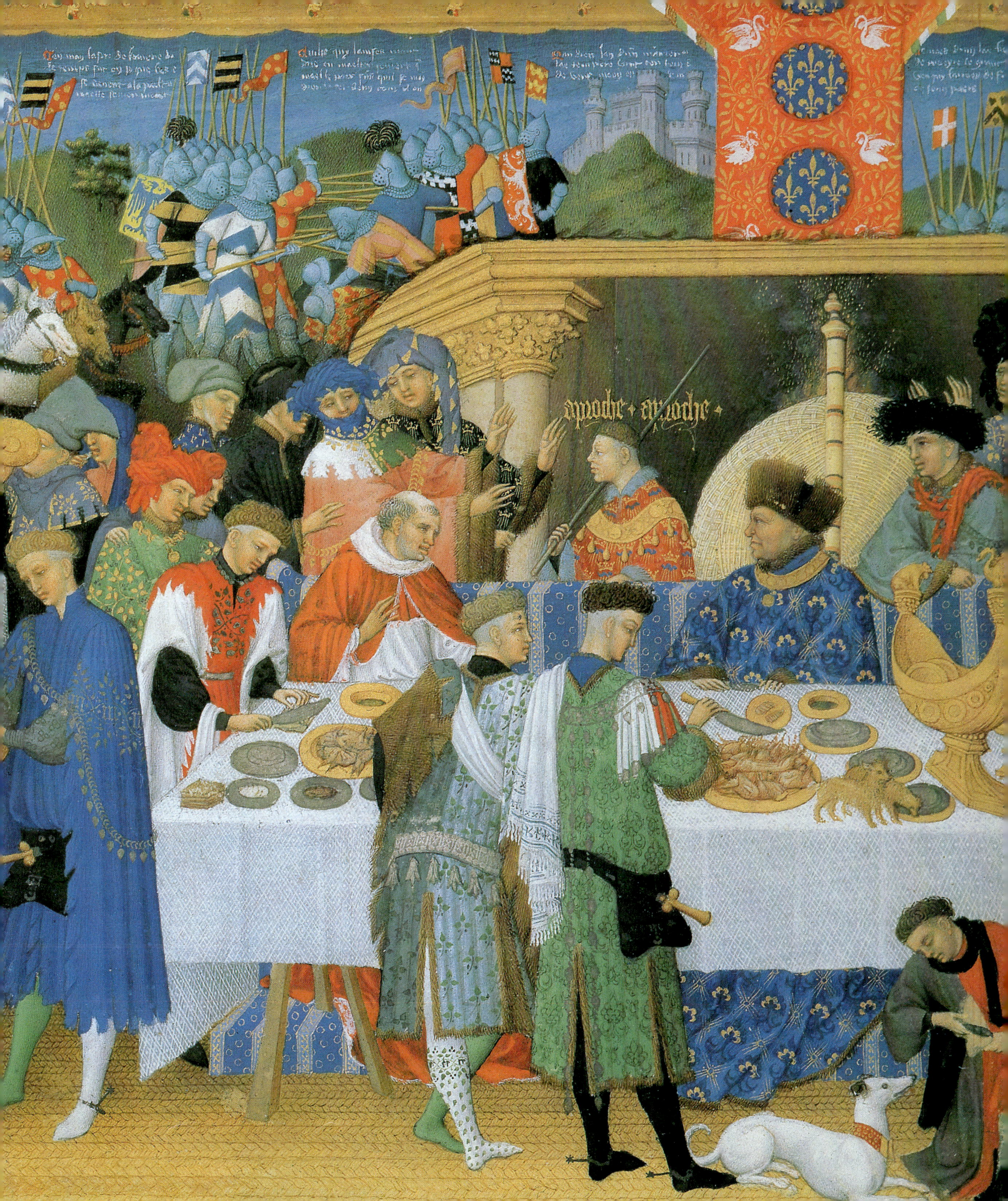
aproche aproche

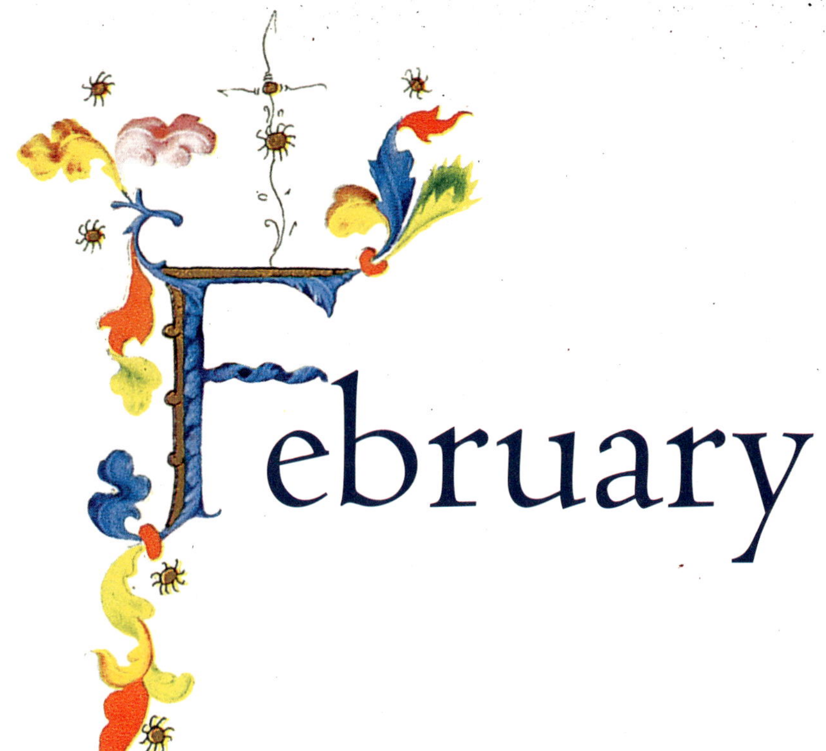

February

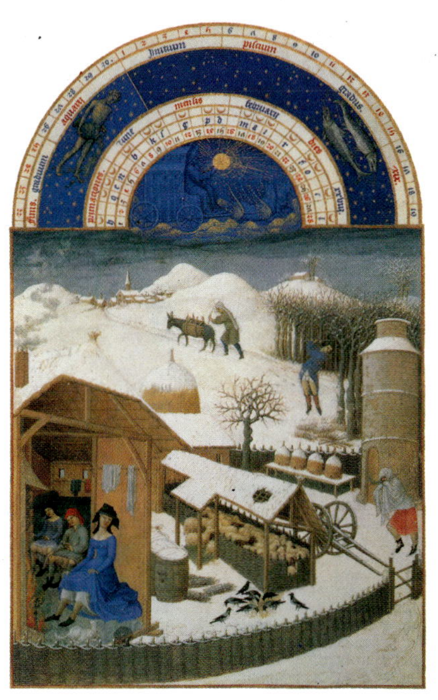

The enemy in February is the bitter cold of winter, and here we are looking, not at a rich man's castle, but at a modest farm. There, in the warmest place, right in front of the open fire, is the lady of the house. She thinks she is quite alone, but we can see her, shyly lifting her dress to warm her knees. Behind her are a farm-hand and a maidservant, too poor to wear underwear and also quite unaware that we can see them! Outside the house there is still some shelter to be found, with all the sheep out of the cold, and the birds being fed. The bees are safe, too, in their hives, and all around there is a fence. In front of the dovecote a figure is running towards the warmth inside — no wonder that she is freezing, she hasn't even got stockings on. Two other men are outside the fence, gathering firewood, and beyond them is the great snow-covered world. We hope that everybody out there is protected from the bitter cold and sense — how lucky we are to have a warm home.

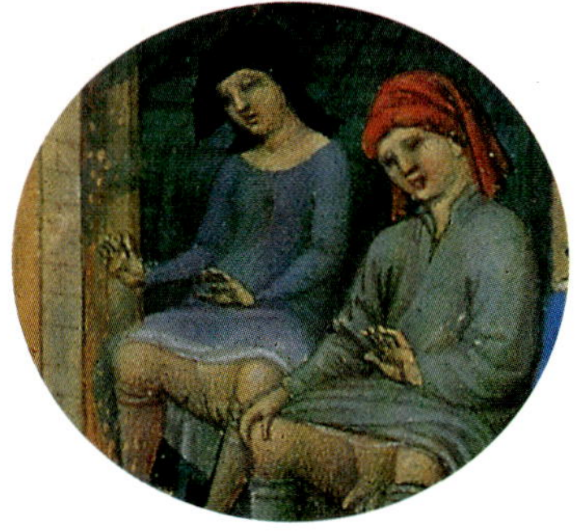

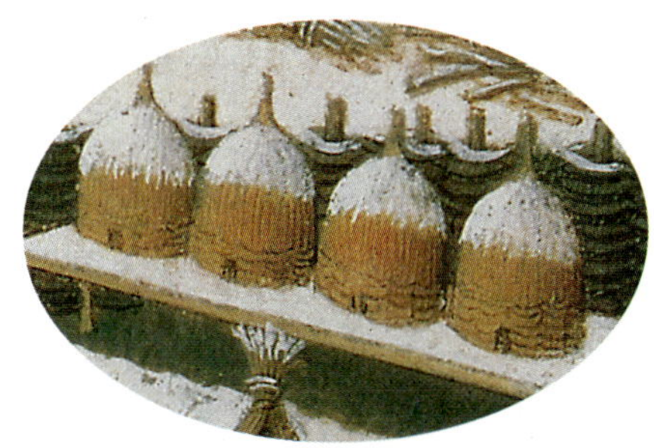

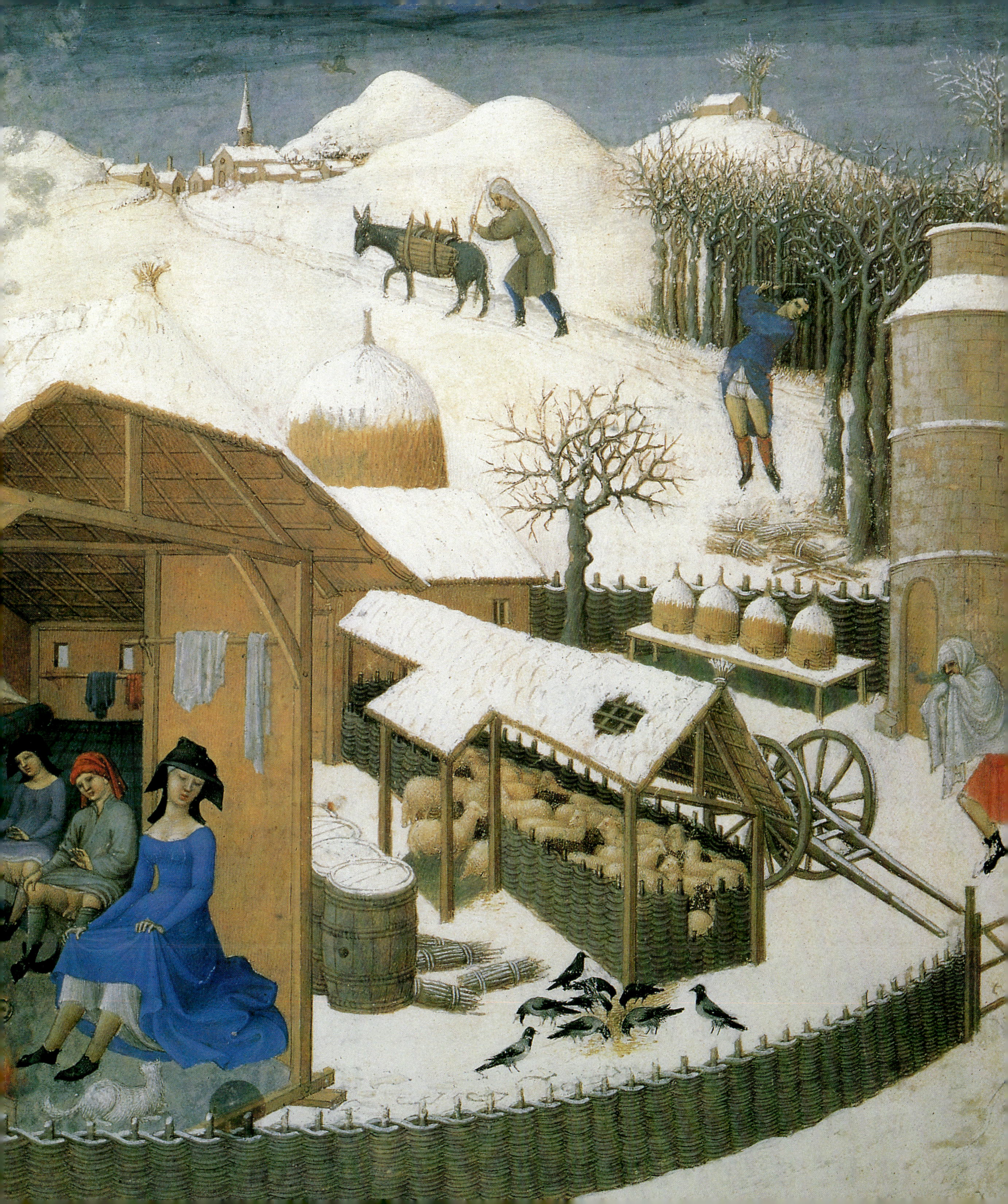

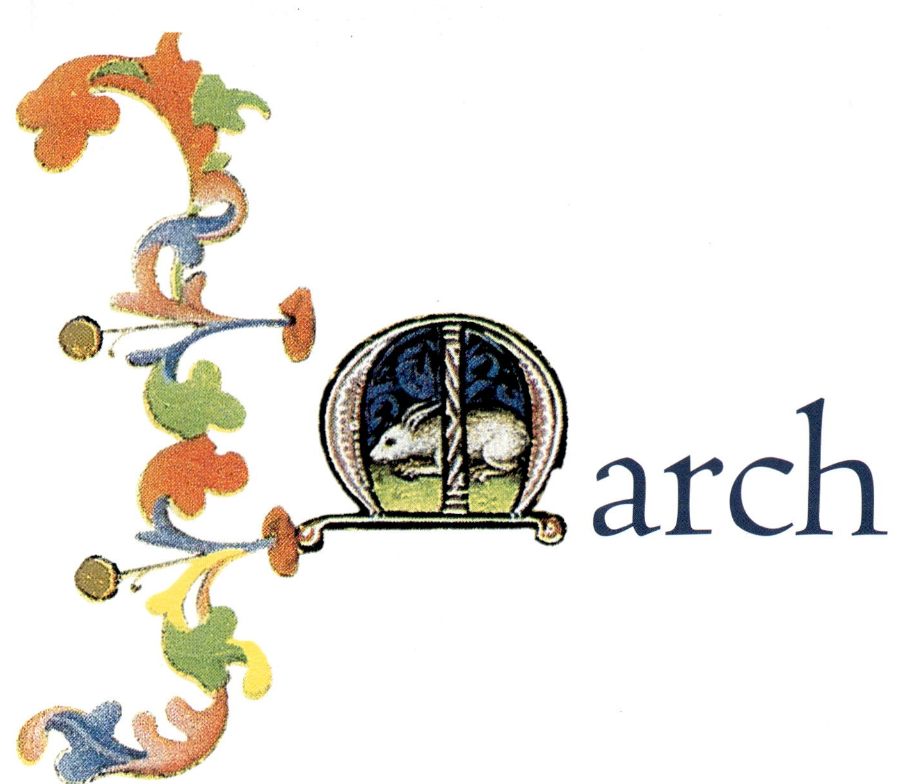

March

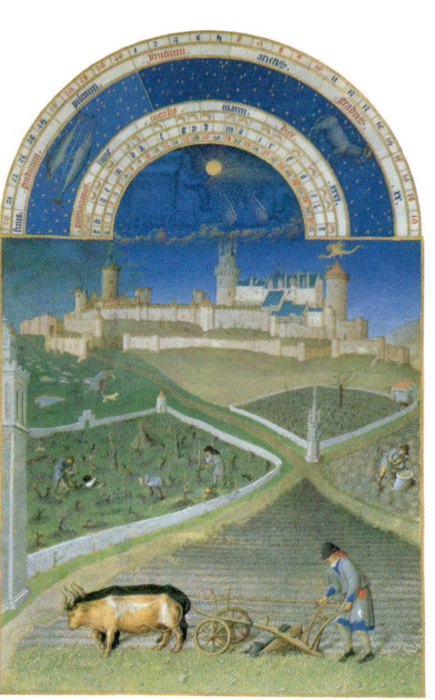

By March, the snow has gone and all the peasants, who work for the duke, are hard at work. The shepherd is getting grass for the sheep, others are pruning the vines, which means cutting them back so that they will grow better when the sun shines. One man is ploughing with his oxen, another sifting grain for sowing. The countryside looks alive: only the castle shows no signs of activity. It is like the carved boundary stone where the four roads meet, a wonderful thing marking the duke's land, but it does not seem to belong. Who has the better time, the men who are really doing something, or those shut away in the lovely castle? Which matters more, the stone sculpture or the little tree that stands behind it and attracts the birds?

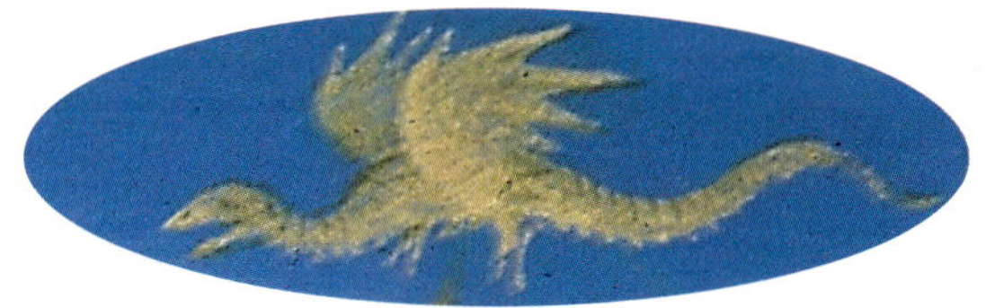

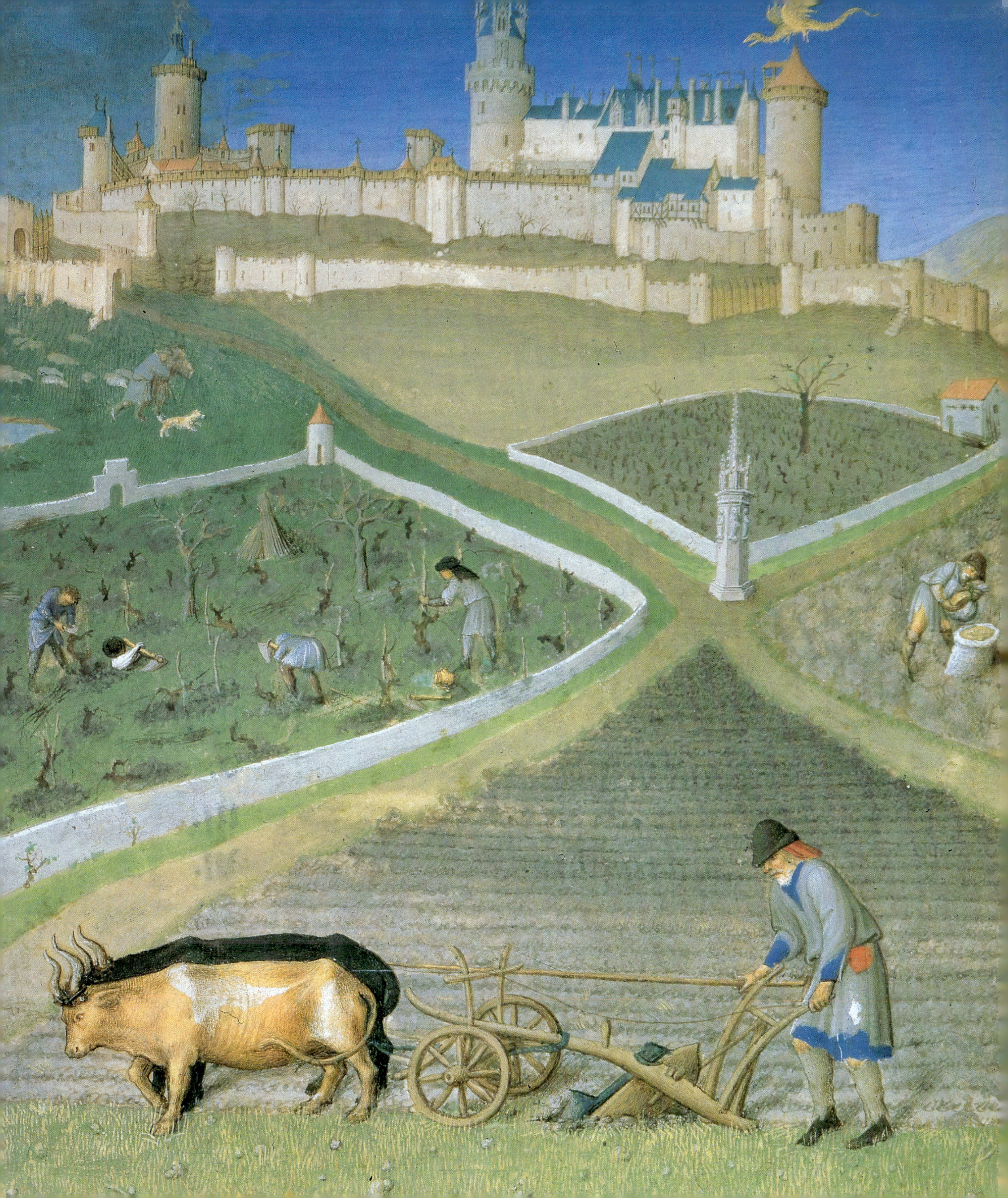

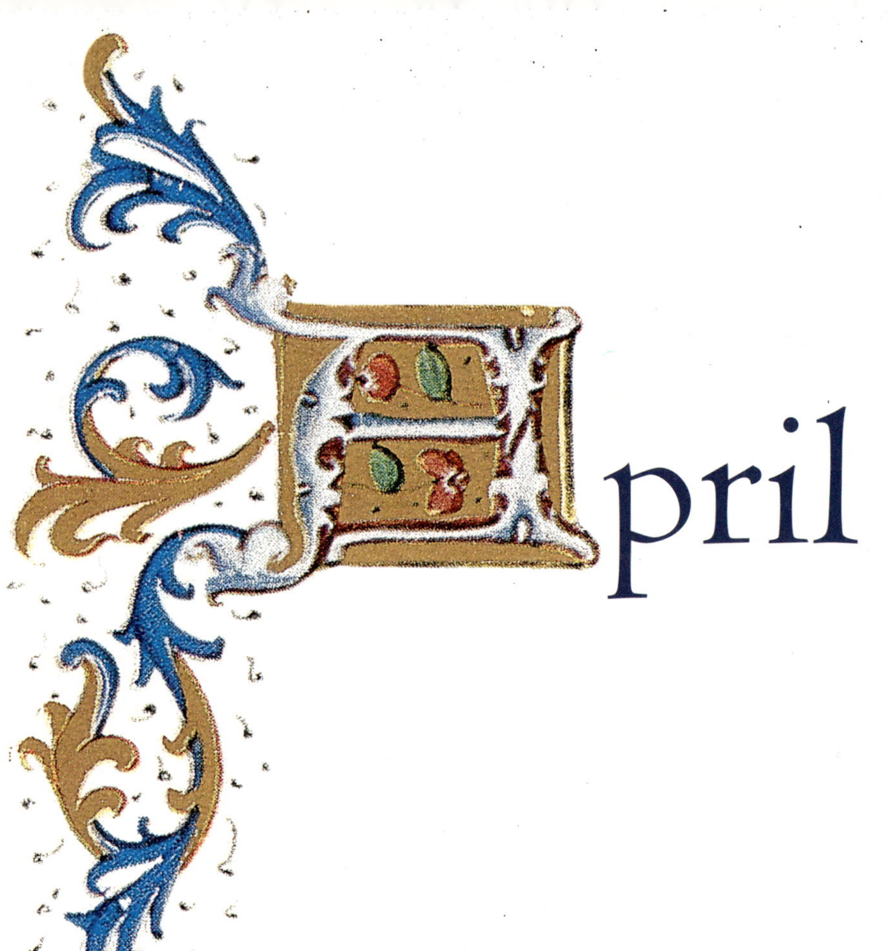

April

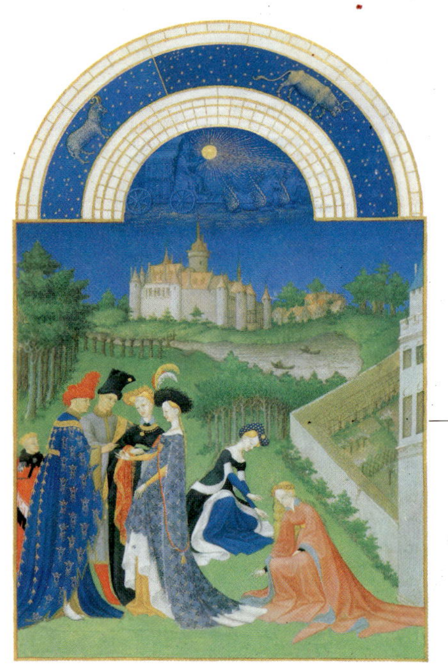

April is the time for picking flowers — and for getting engaged. The orchard is rich with blossom, and we hope that the lovely young bride in blue and her groom will have that kind of life together, full of sunshine and flowers. Even the castle, one of the duke's many castles, is more homey, with a little village under its wing. The two boats on the lake are fishing together; they have a net hung between them to catch fish for the duke's table. They can only do this if they help each other and pull their weight, which again reminds us of marriage. Both have to try if it is to work. It might not look like it, but everybody on this sunlit world is doing something. The ladies who have no partners yet, are searching for flowers, and even the little boy at the side is learning what grownup life is like.

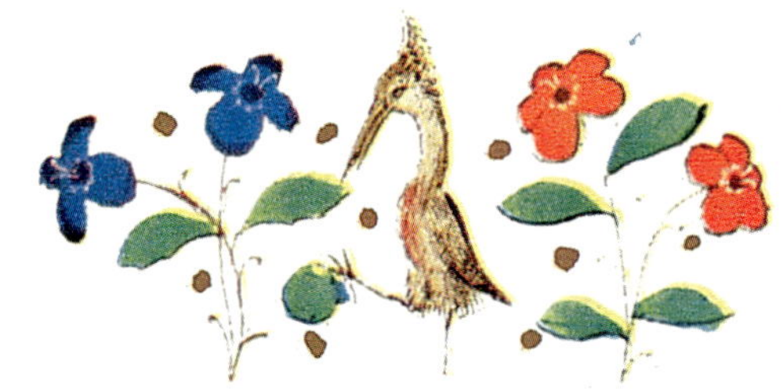

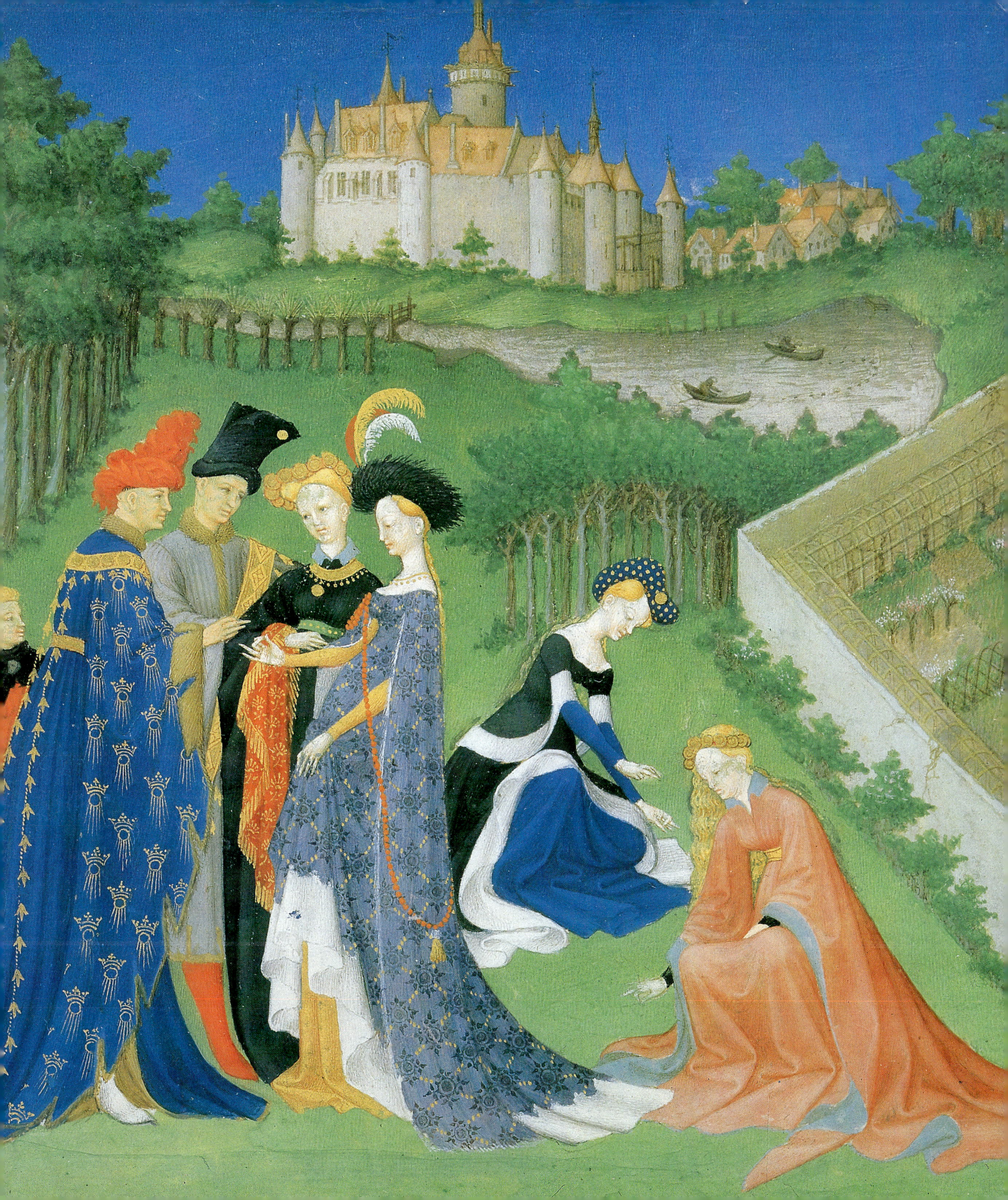

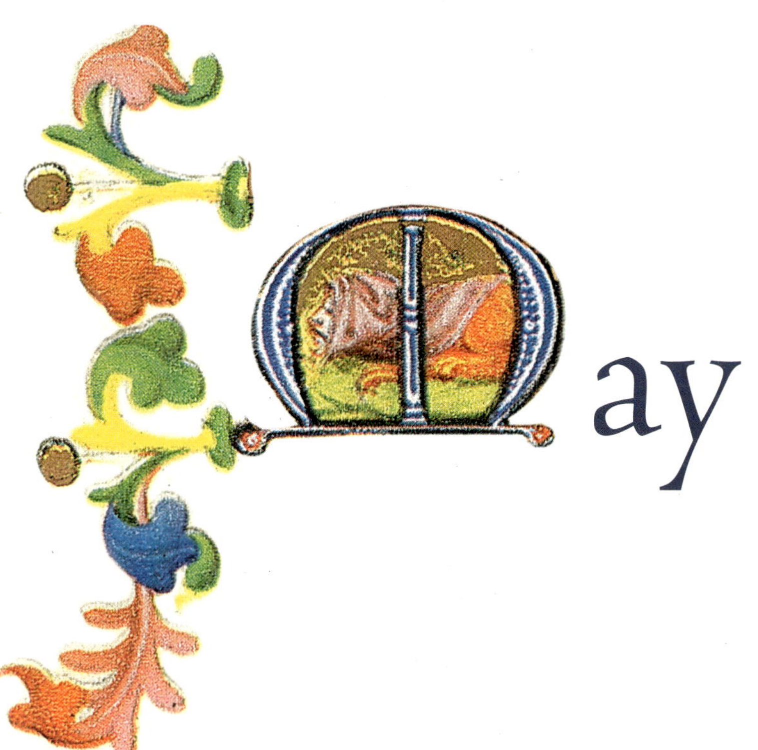

ay

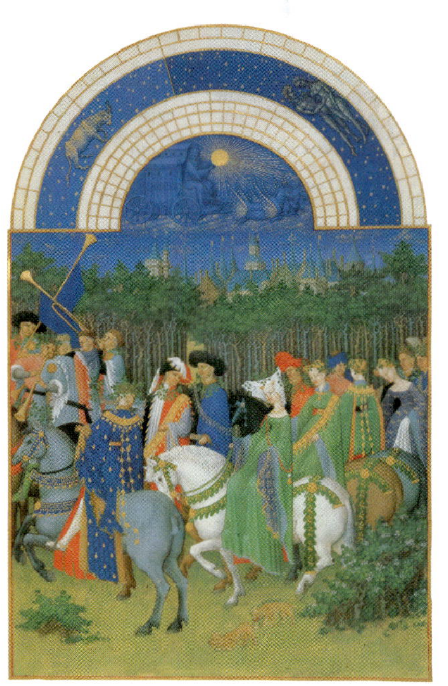

In May, the duke is riding in the open air. We can only see him from behind here, but he is still wearing the same kind of rich blue and gold clothes that he wore for the New Year, and there are his two tiny dogs again. He has a whole band playing music for him and some very pretty girls, but nobody looks all that happy. They are not talking to one another, except for the two at the back. They have all put wreathes of greenery on their heads or around their necks since green is the colour of May. The wild rose tree is flowering beside them, but for all the wonderful colours, there is a sort of shut-in feeling. The castle looms above the forest, but there does not appear to be much space. All those sweet-faced girls look downwards, as was expected of them in those times. The artists enjoy the spectacle, very much so, but they are doubtful about it. Better to look on than actually to take part!

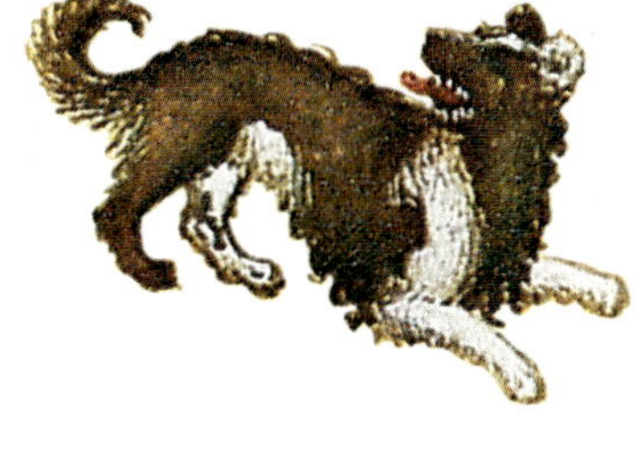

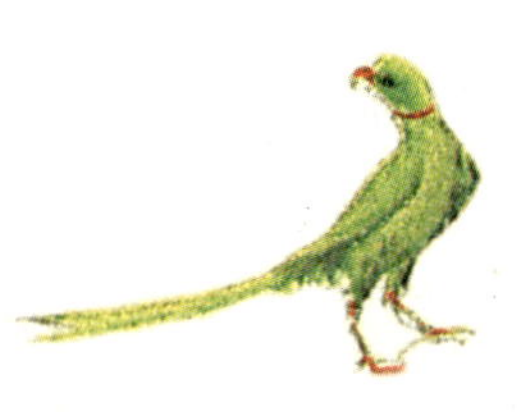

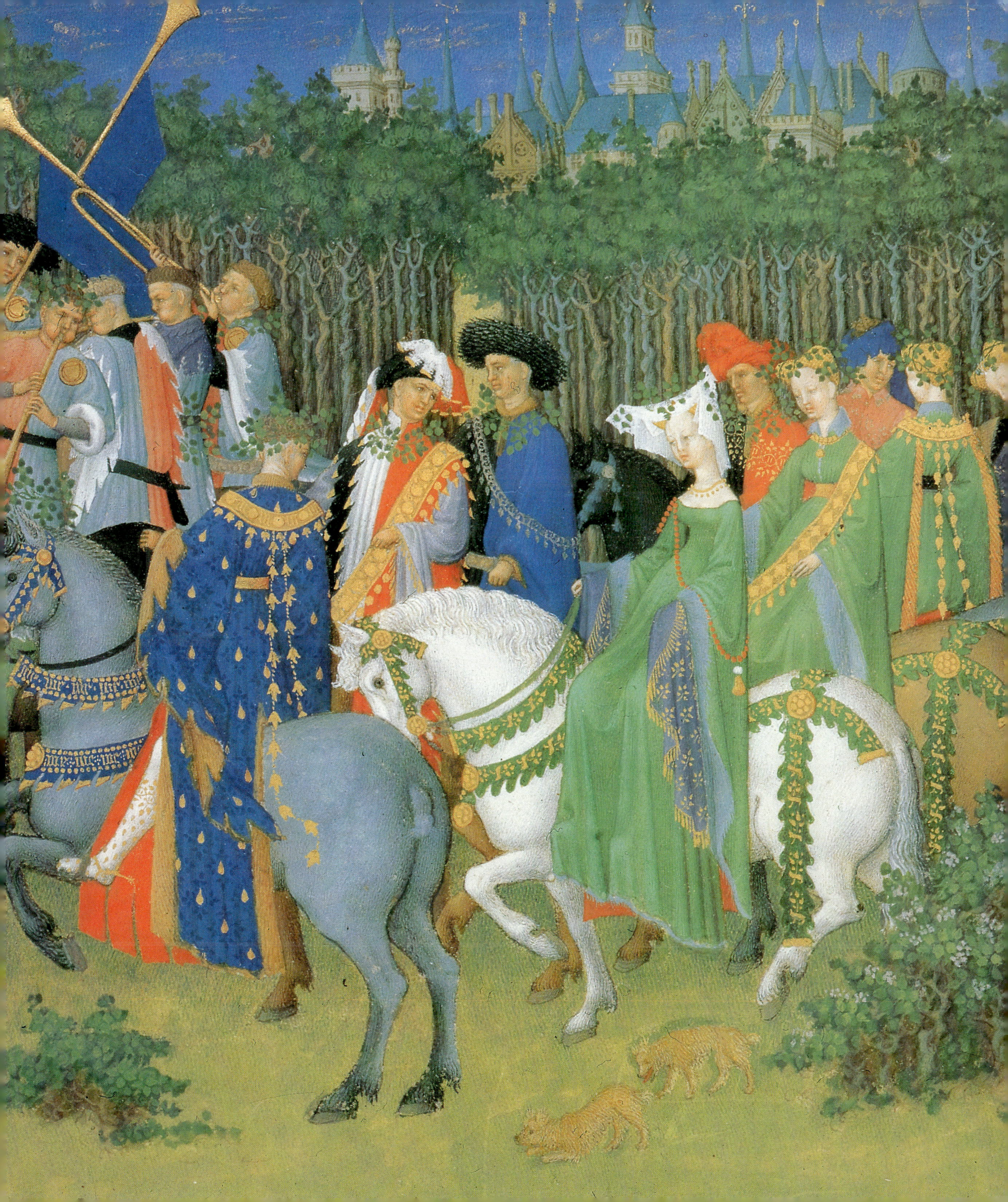

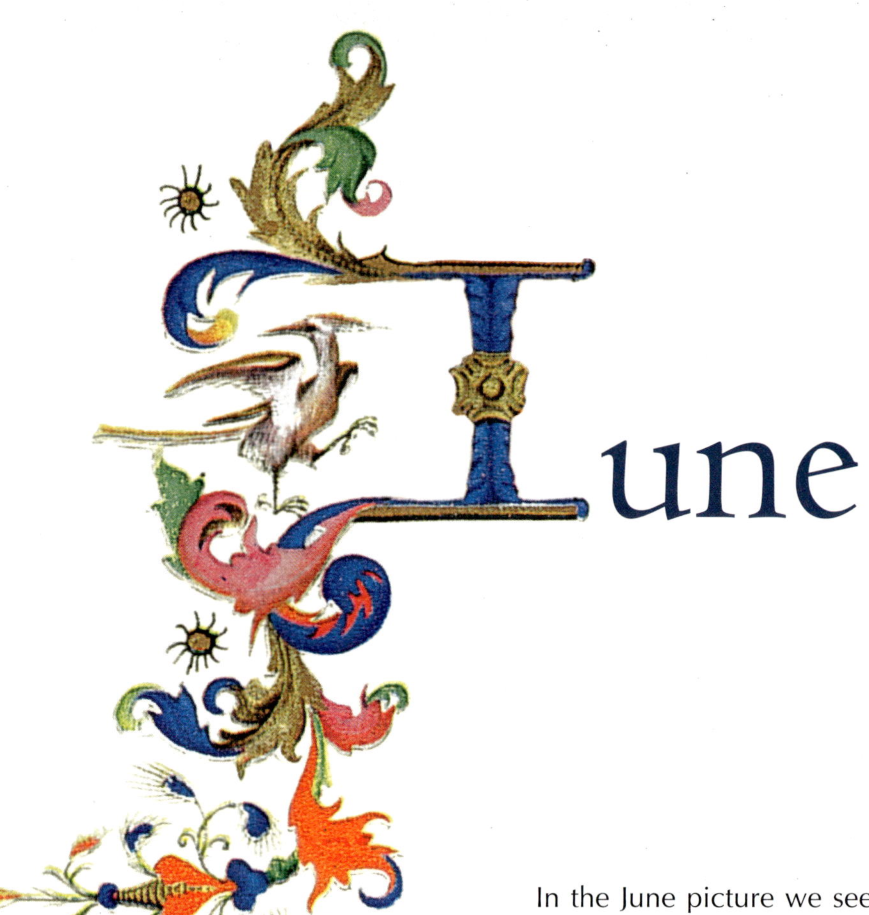

June

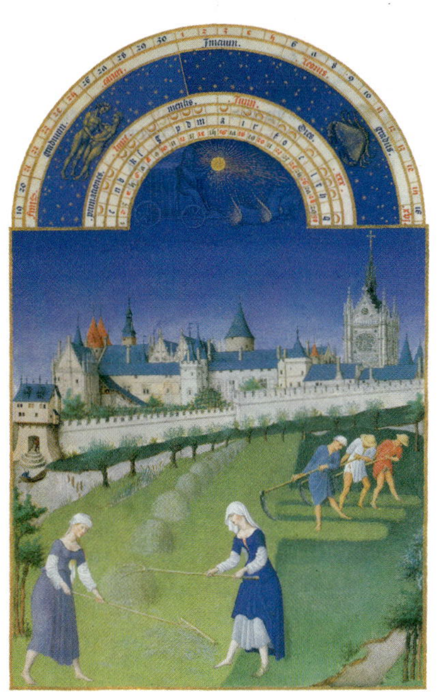

In the June picture we see more clearly the same castle that was peeping out behind the trees in May. This time there are even people in it, going up the steps and looking out of the windows. It used to stand on the banks of the River Seine, just outside Paris, and the tall, elegant church we can see on the right, the famous "Sainte-Chapelle", is actually still there today.

The castle seems to be in a little world of its own, complete with high wall, while outside, in the other world, the peasants make hay. They are making hay while the sun shines, men and a woman sharing the job, all swinging their sickles or forks vigorously, with hats and scarfs to protect them from the sun. The girls are looking at each other as it might be time for a break, and the man in the middle, with great strong legs, looks as if he, too, would much prefer to sit under the trees or cool off in the stream. Around the meadow flows the Seine, and the water is so clean that we can see the fish swimming in it. If the castle folks are enclosed by their wall, so are the haymakers enclosed by their river: two different worlds, but both with their good sides.

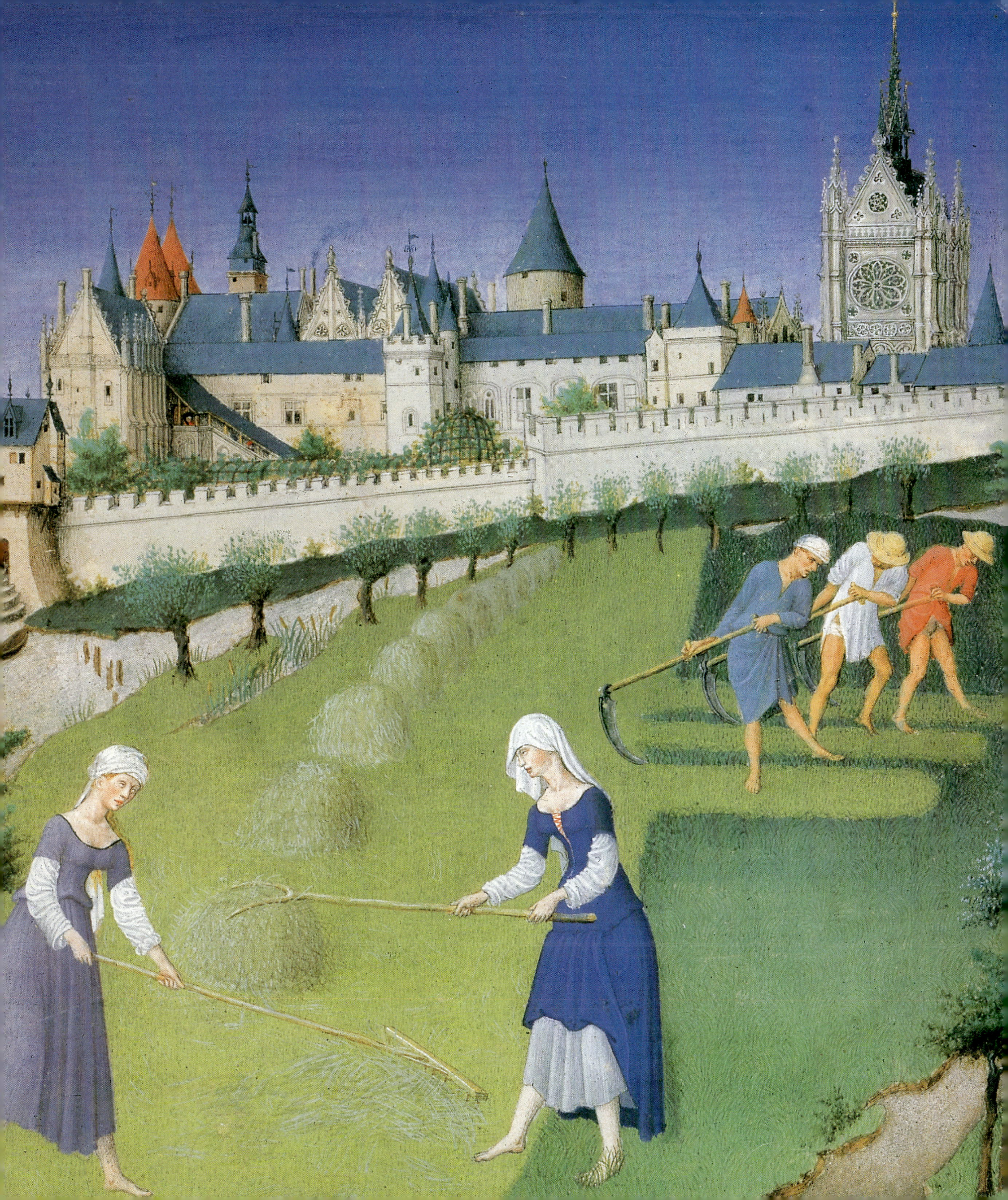

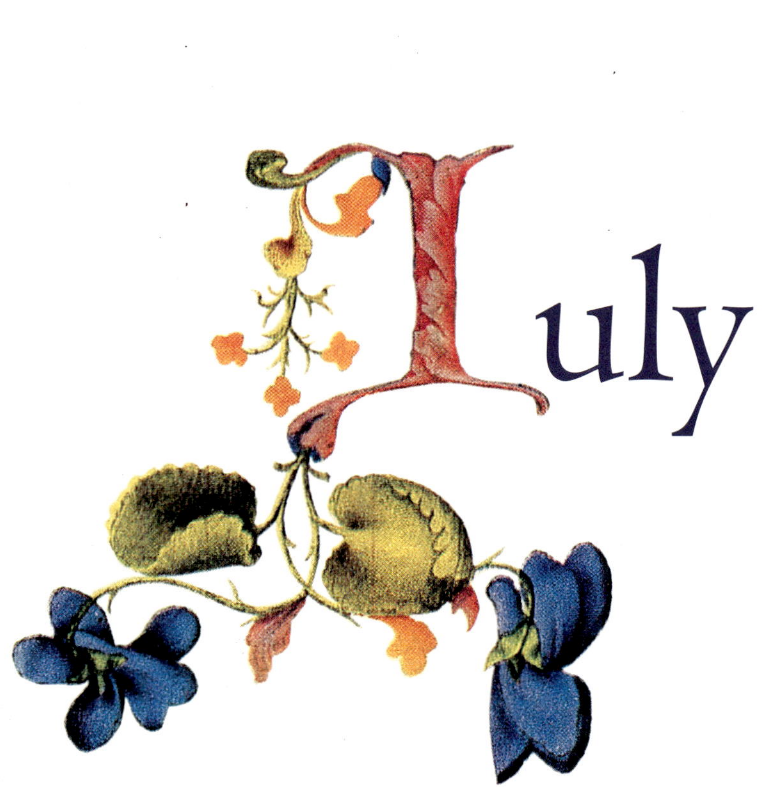

July

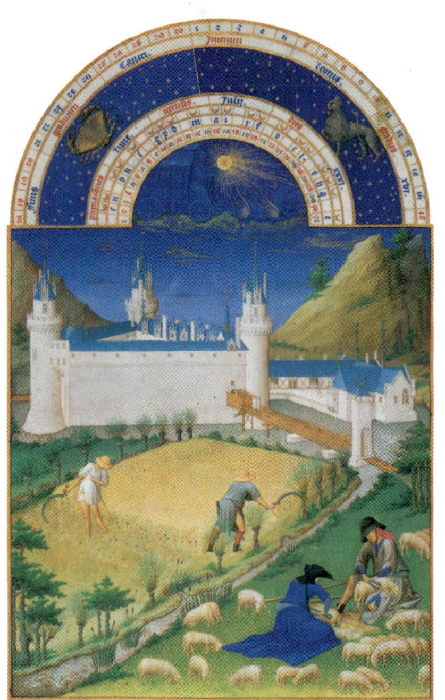

In July the wheat is being harvested and the sheep are being shorn. The lady at the front is the same one as in February's picture, except that now she is hot and has rolled up her sleeves. Everybody wears whatever clothes they want and nobody overdoes it at work. Peacefully and happily, they are all getting on with the job. This castle is again very cut off from the workers. There is an almost blank wall, and the bridge over the moat is very narrow. But the four peasants are quite unconcerned. They might watch the swans if they drift along the stream towards them, but they are not interested in the high, white castle. They like what they are doing, and they know how to do it well; they are fortunate people. No one is getting hurt here, no one is being lazy, no one is being envious, no one is being silly. It is a nice world.

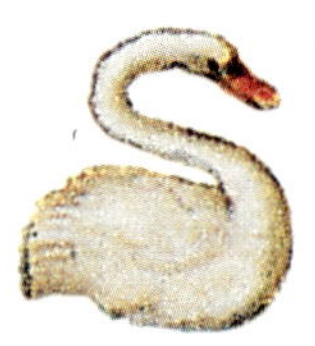

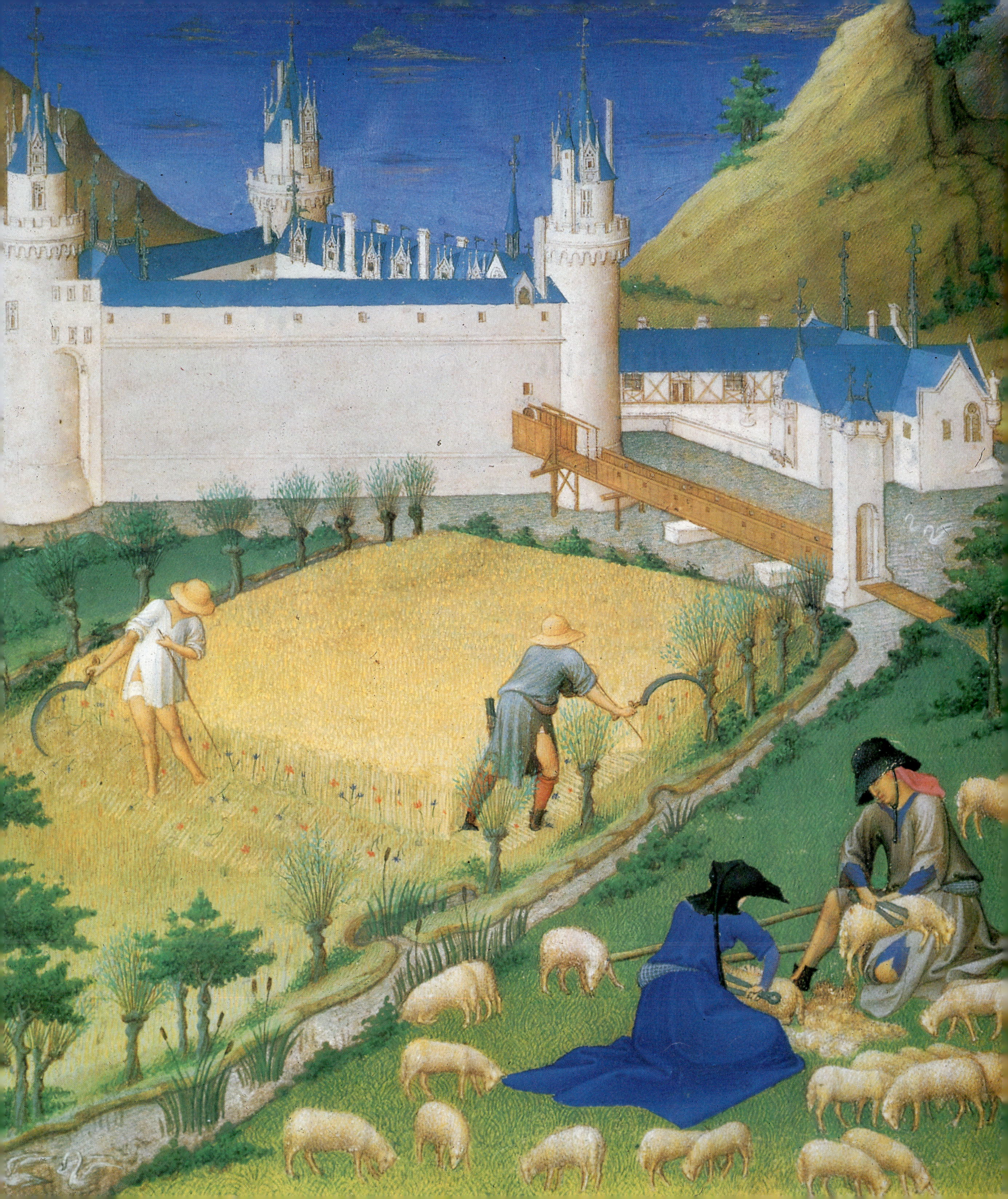

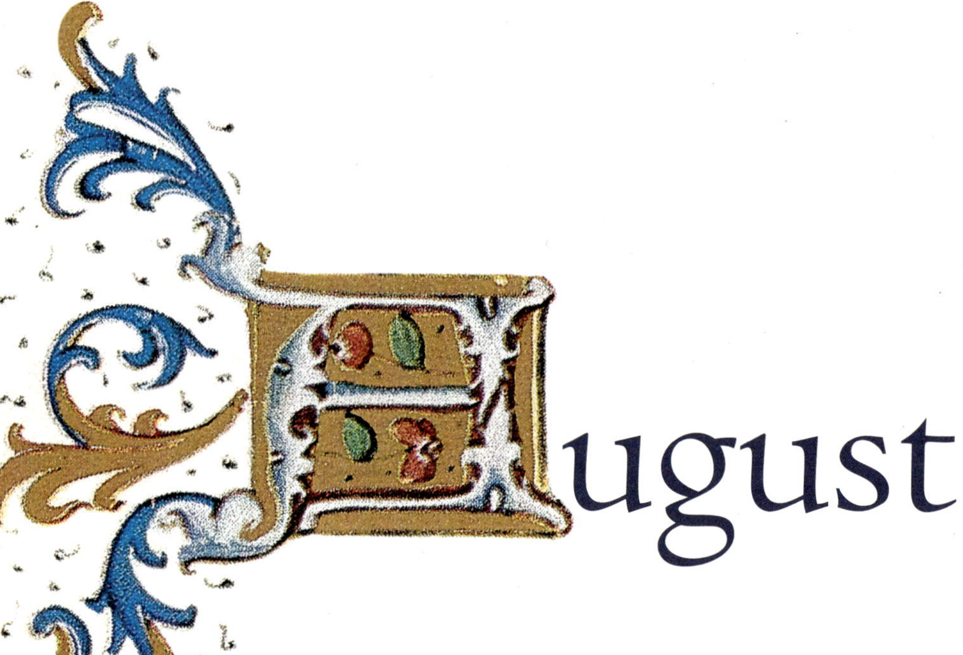

August

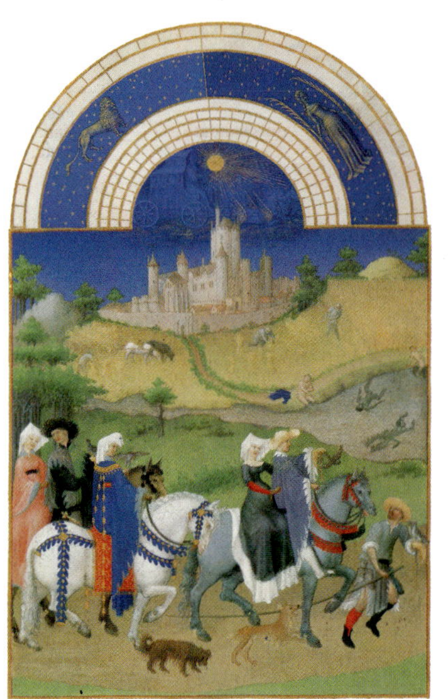

In August, the world of the castle and the world of the peasant almost meet. Nobles and ladies have come hunting, with their falcons, birds carefully trained to kill their prey and bring it back to the huntsman. Meanwhile the peasants are finishing the harvest and loading the haycarts. When they want a break, they enjoy a swim, even though none of them has a bathing suit. We might think at first that the rich people on horseback have an easier life, but look how tight their clothes are, in all this heat. They have special rules of behaviour which they have to keep, however little sense it makes. They do not look free. But the poor people have the satisfaction of doing their job well, and then having the even greater satisfaction of being able to swim and get cool. Things are sometimes not quite what they seem at first.

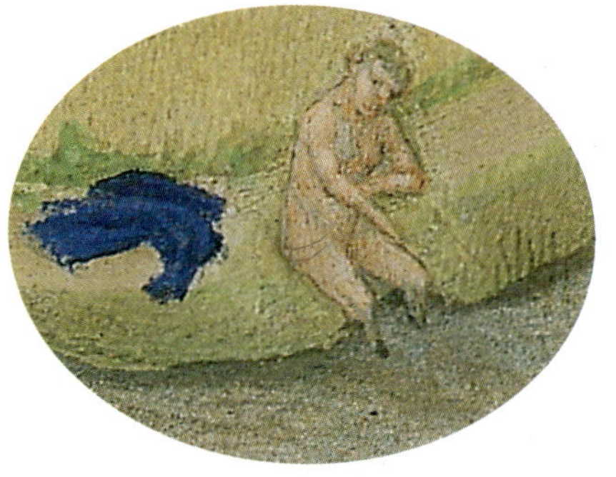

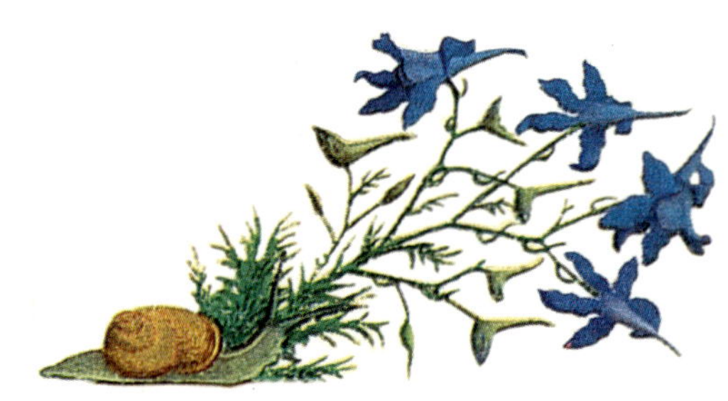

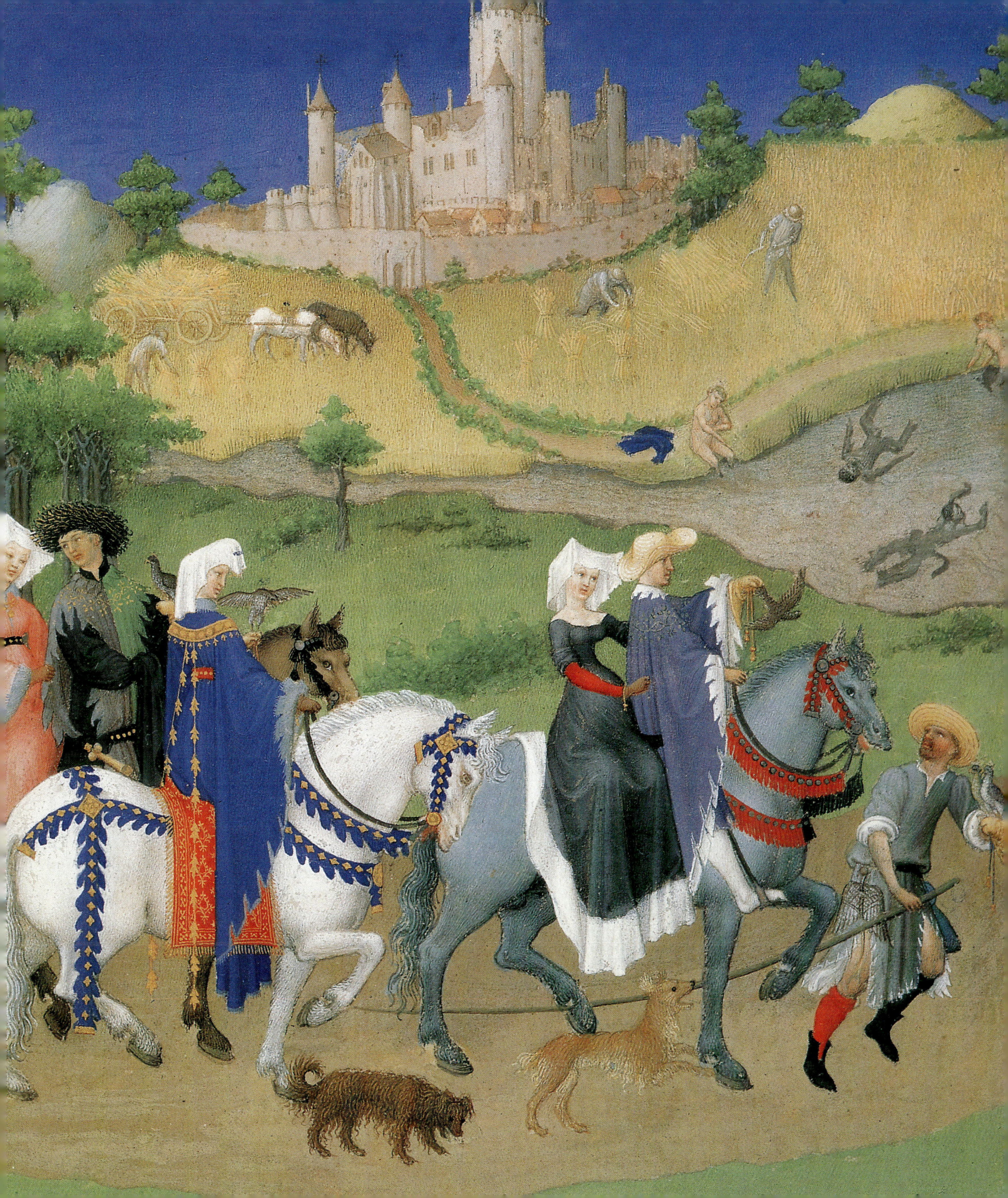

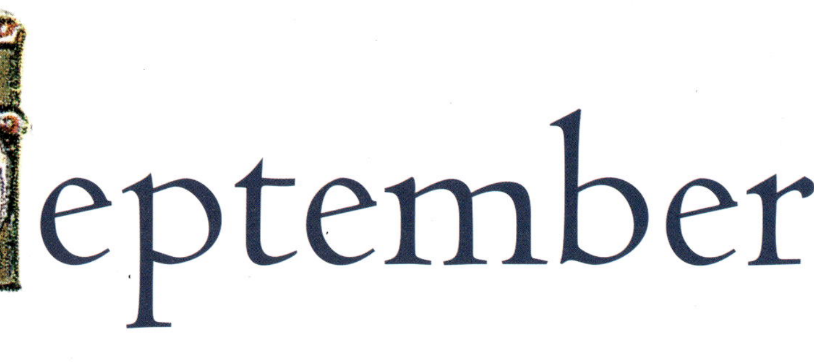

September

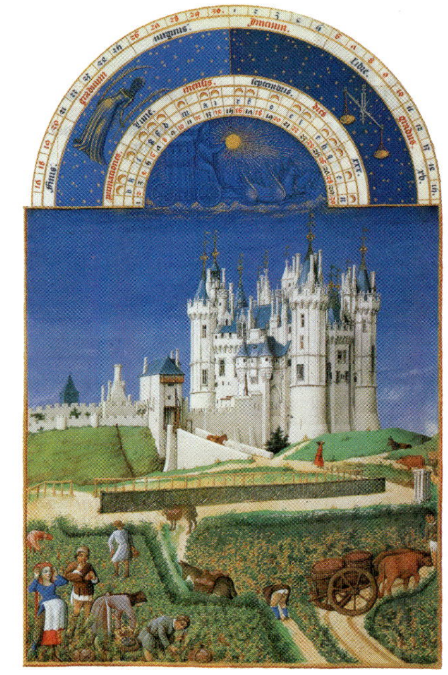

September is the time for gathering in the grapes, and, as we can see from the man in the brown shirt, for tasting them, too. The colours now have become richer and deeper. There is the purple of the grapes and the darker blue of the sky. The castle seems more open, too. A girl in a glowing autumn-coloured dress is carrying her basket towards it, and a fine horse gallops down as if to greet her. It is a life where animals and people work in harmony with one another, all doing their share. Even the castle, with different animals apparently moving towards it, seems to be the place where the grapes will be stored and made into wine. The vineyard, with all its various colours and workers and activities, is as interesting to our eye as the fairy tale castle with its little towers and pinnacles. And to make it more human, the artists have painted, on the left, the funny looking tower that is really the chimney kitchen. This is a delightfully earthy picture.

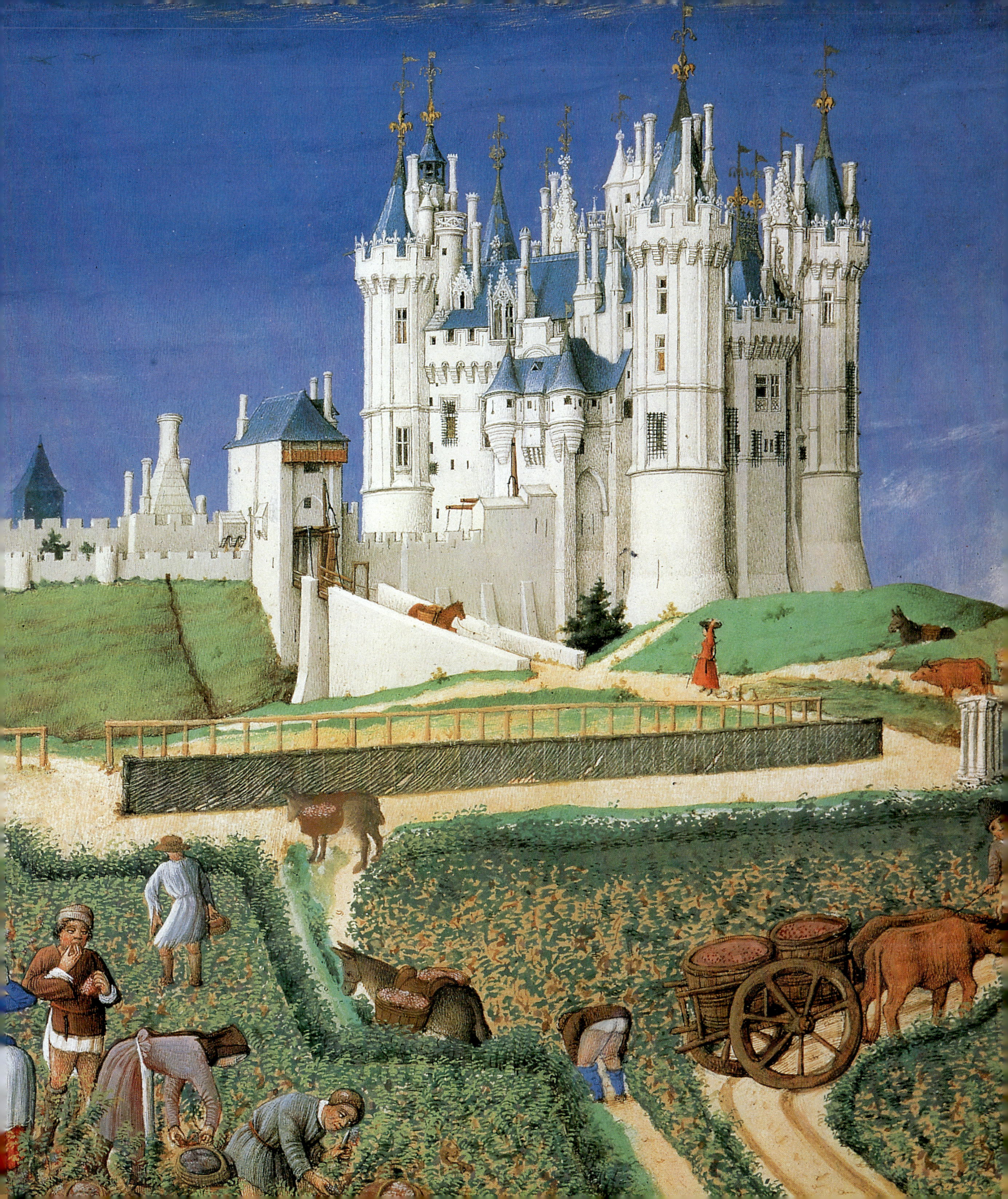

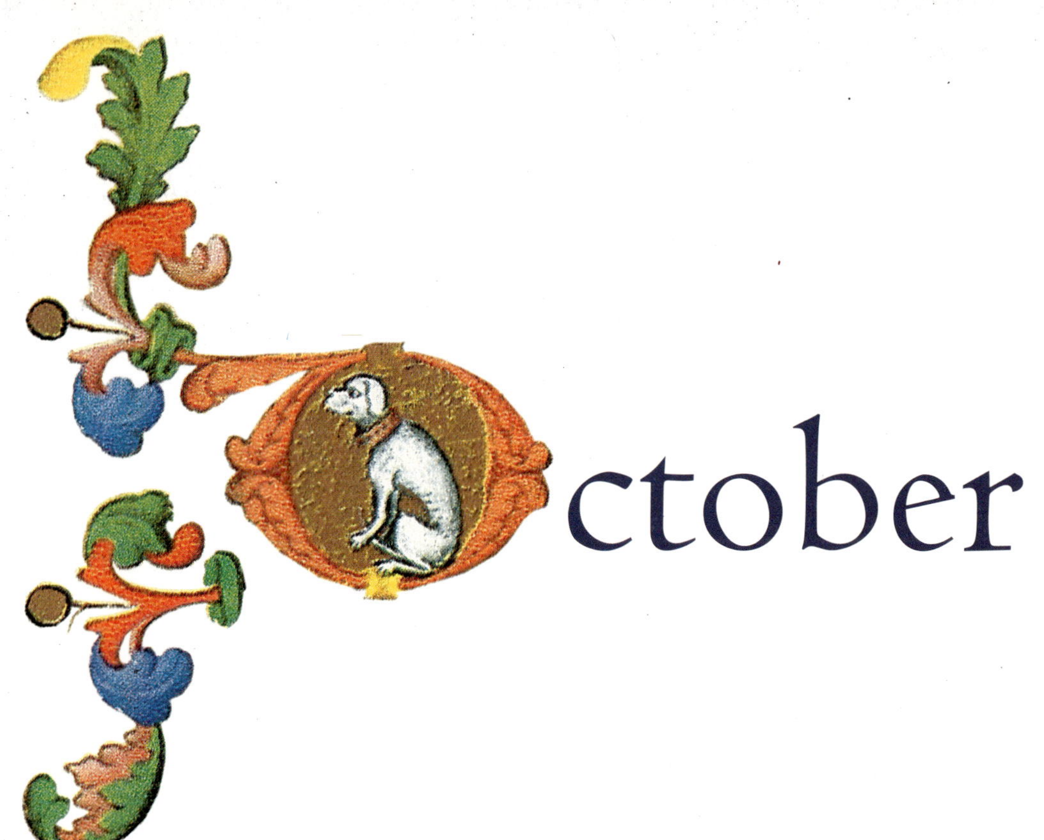

October

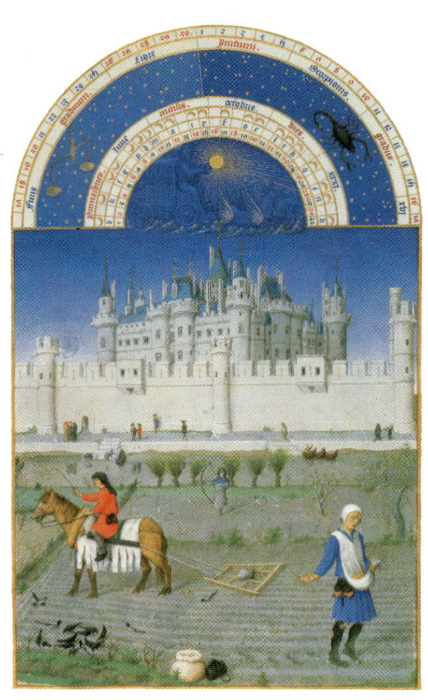

In October we are outside Paris again, dominated by the huge building in the centre — the former palace of the kings of France — that will one day be called the Louvre. There are men and women strolling on the banks of the river Seine, but the main concern of the artist is to show that this is the time for sowing. One man, on a horse, drags the harrow, which makes furrows in which the other man can sow the seed. Neither of them looks very happy, maybe because, despite the scarecrow in the middle, dressed as an archer, the magpies are having a fine time stealing the corn. The fishermen are busy, too, but all those people just chatting in the background give the whole scene an air of leisure. No attention is being paid to the sowers, not even by the skinny little dogs on the river bank. Perhaps the most important shape in the whole picture is the round bag at the very bottom. It is as creamy white as the castle itself, but its open mouth reminds us that without sowing seed for the coming year our open mouths will not be filled. The sower's apron with its full pocket of seed is like a full stomach. Perhaps that is what he is dreaming of — his next satisfying dinner?

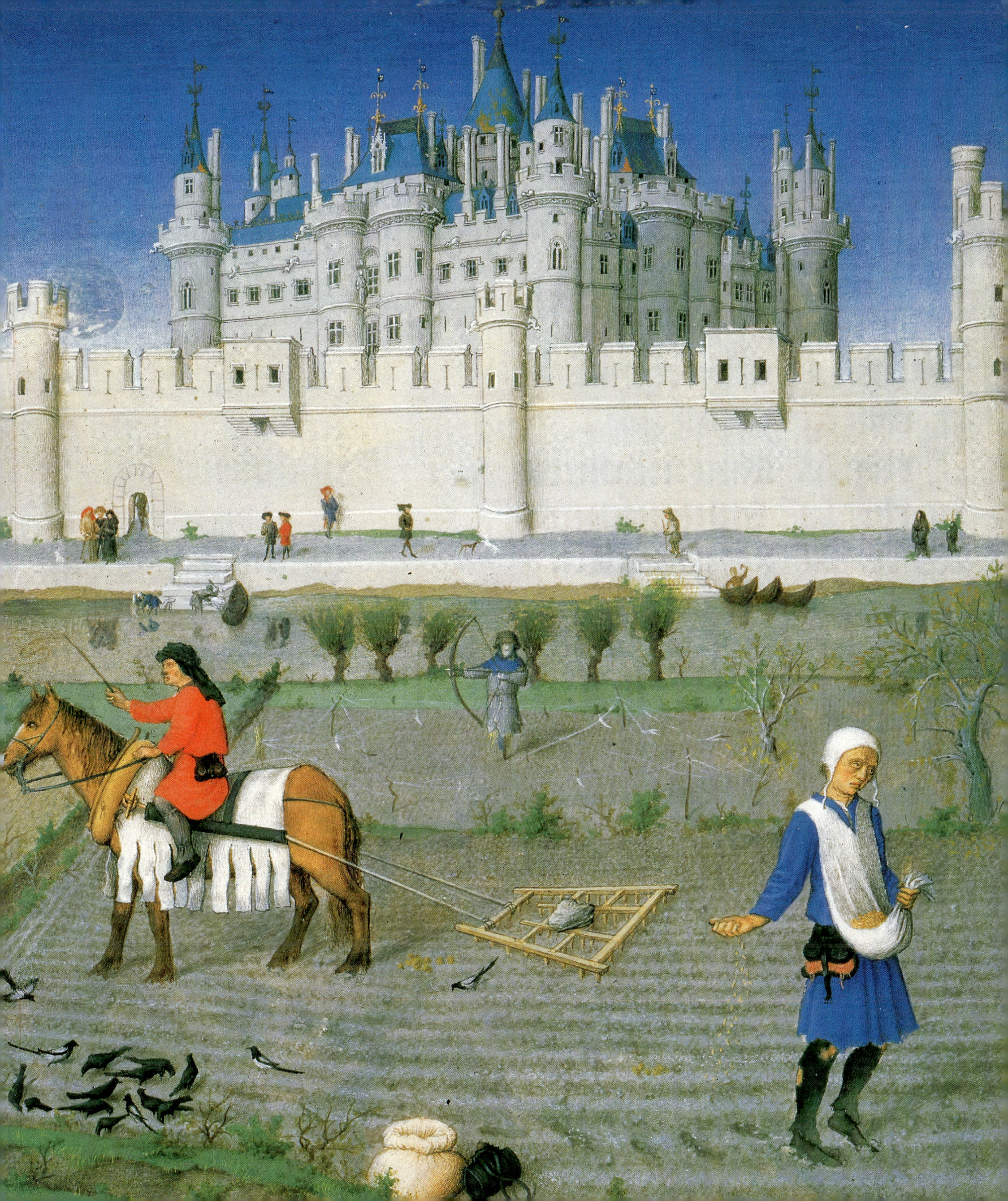

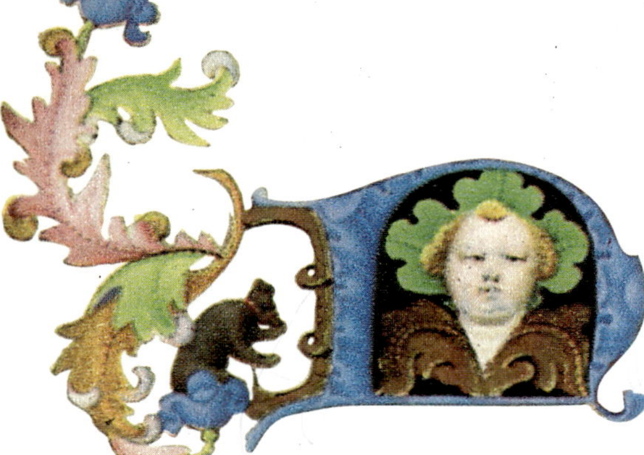

November

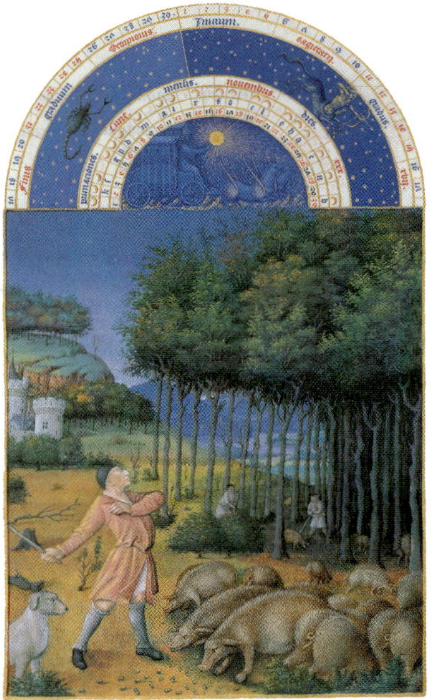

In November, the peasants harvest the acorns to feed their pigs. Pigs are very important to them, as we can see. The biggest and strongest of the peasants is throwing his stick up into the trees to knock down more and more acorns for his splendid pigs. He has two men helping him and also a dog with an air of majesty. (If the duke were a dog, he would look like this!) Behind the trees a great valley sweeps away into the far distance, with lakes and rivers and hills and forests. A small castle on the slope of the hill seems far less important than the space and power of nature. Even the pigs are glorious, with their eager eyes and their concentration on the acorns. We can see that the artist really loves the pigs, perhaps more than he does the people. The peasant is making a fine gesture and he has good clothes, but he is not nearly as handsome as the pigs are!

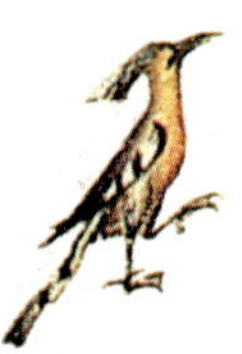

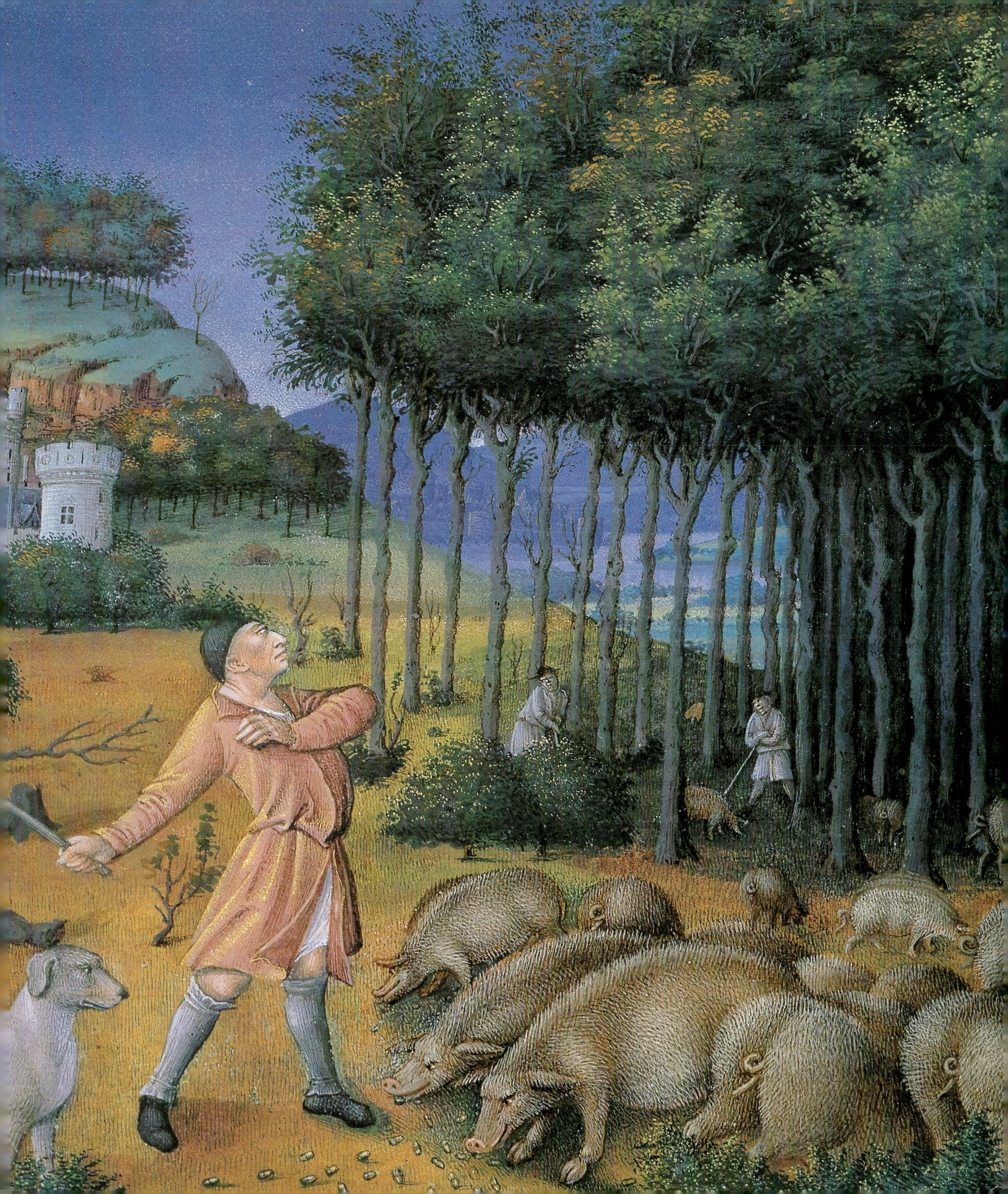

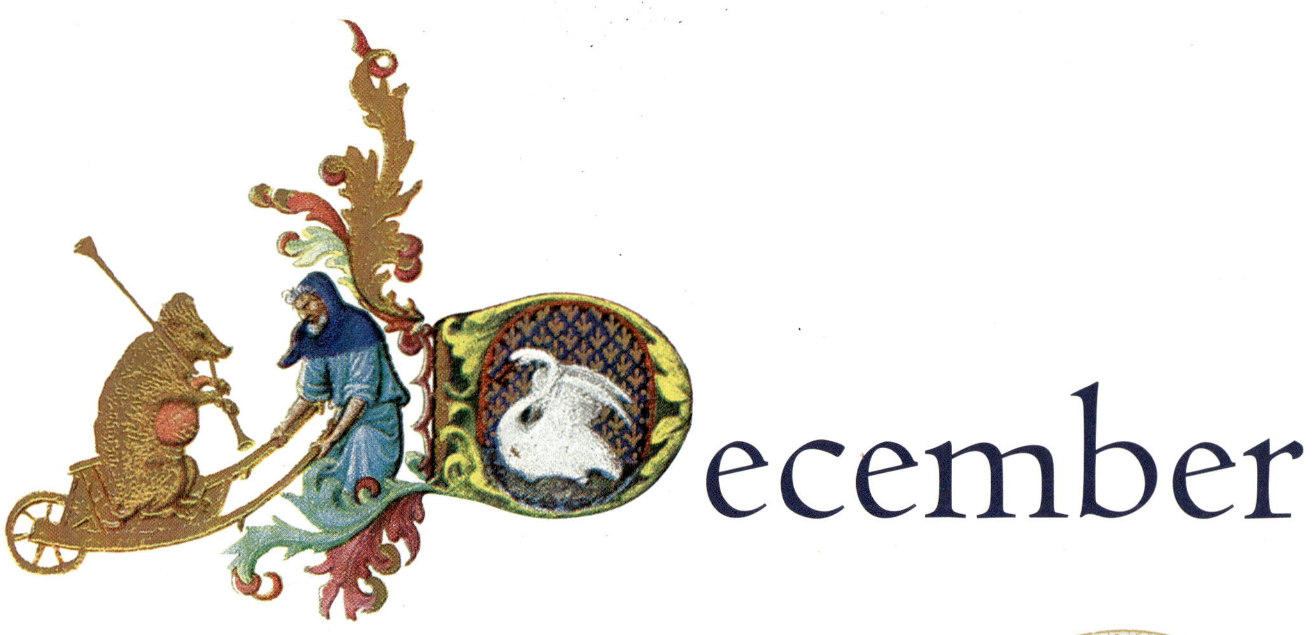

ecember

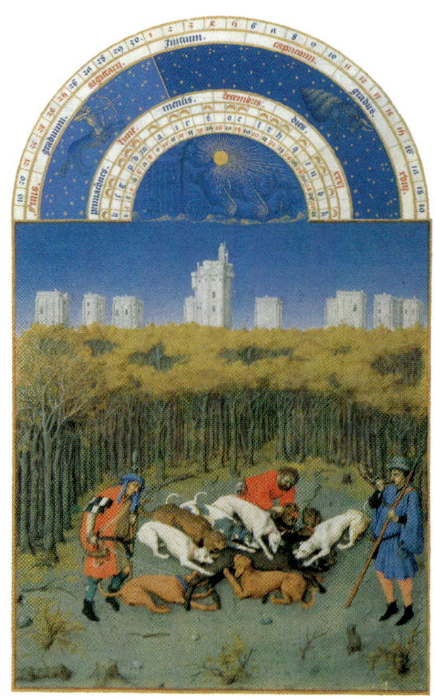

In December the year dies, so the artist decides to finish the Months with a death. It is a hunting death: they have been chasing the wild boar, a very dangerous animal, and now the dogs have cornered him and the chase is over. The huntsmen are trying to call the dogs off: the boar is meant to be for the duke's table. This may be what he will have for his New Year's feast in January. The dogs have had a lovely time and got over-excited, and as for the poor boar, he is dead and his body must be kept safe for the kitchen. The woods are golden with their autumn leaves, the grass has withered, the men are tired and a bit anxious. Only the castle soars silently into the sky, untouched by the seasons. It is a picture about things that end and things that stay the same.

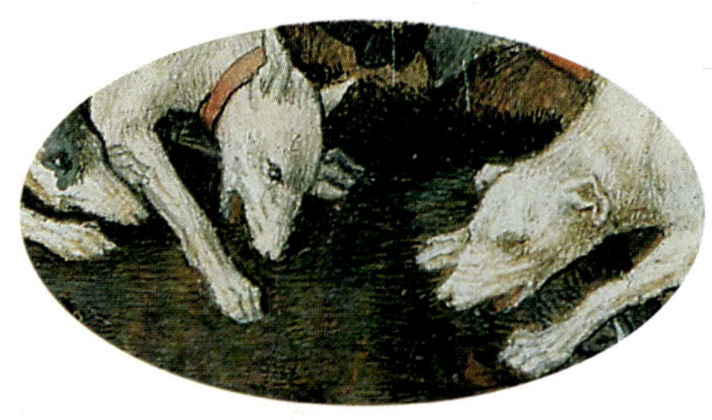

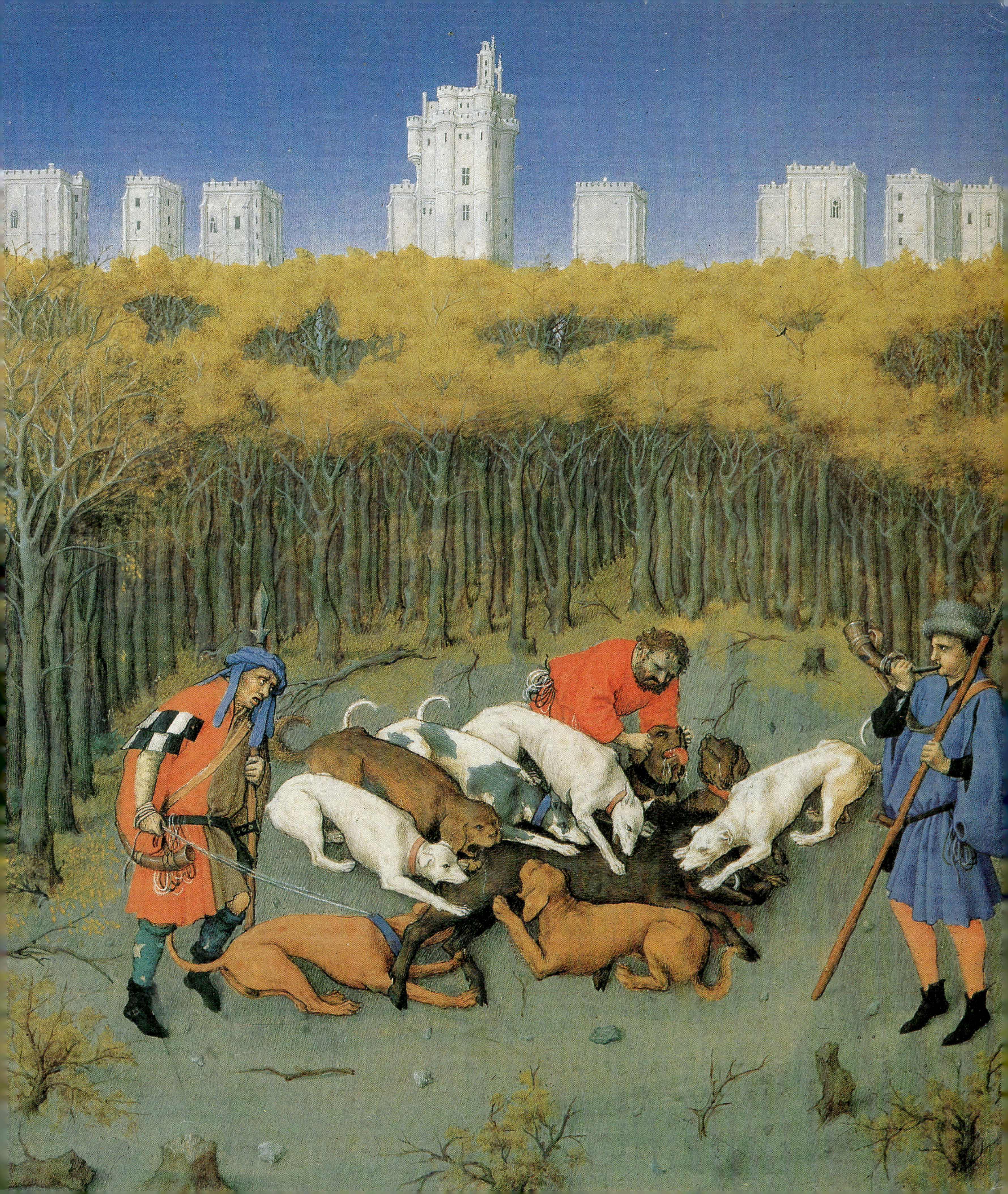

Artists help us to see the glory of the world. They open our eyes to the beauty that we so easily miss. The more we look at these pictures of the Months, the more we shall understand and respond to the wonder of being human.

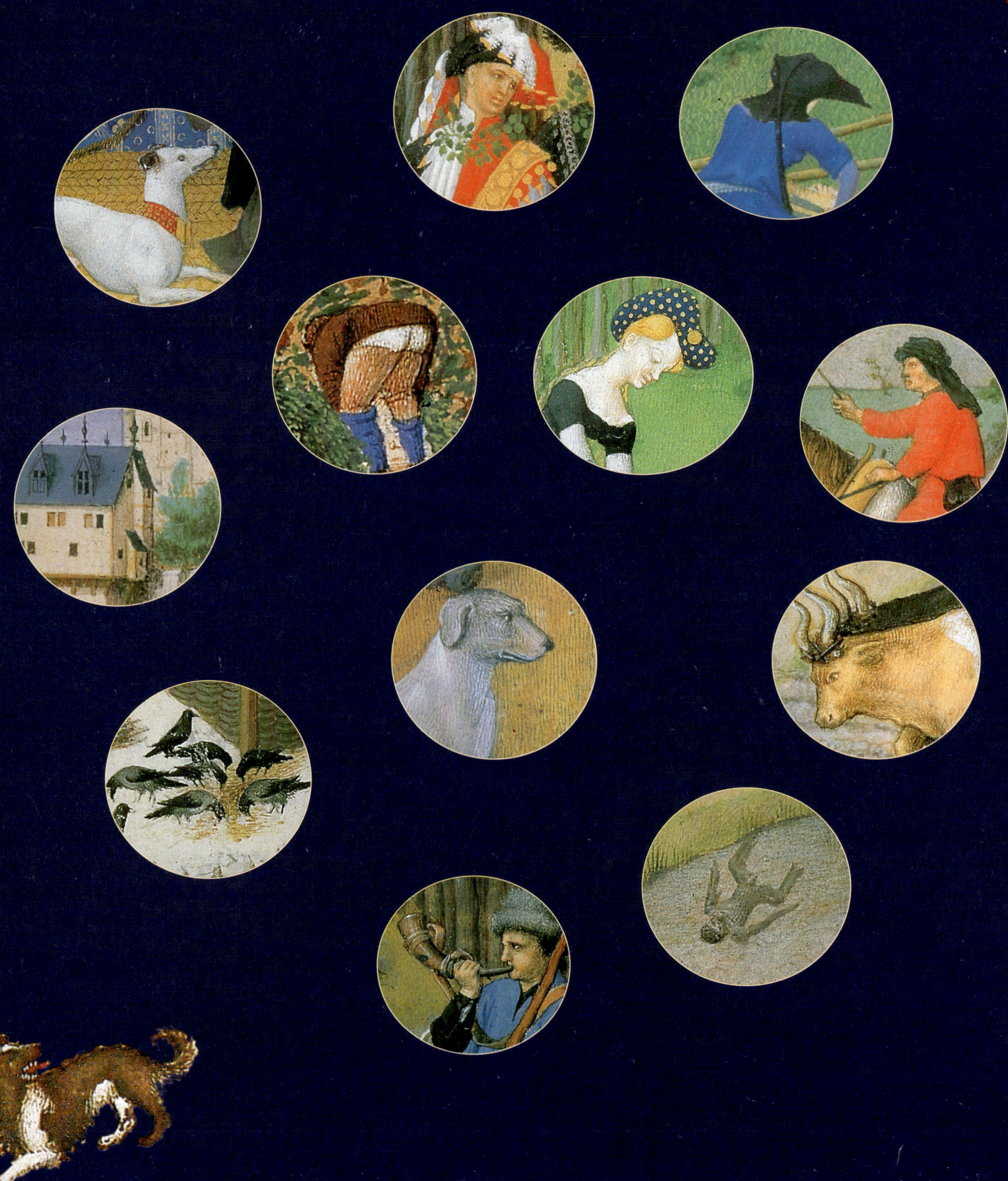